D1739162

PRAISE FOR ALEX LUCAS

Alex Lucas delivers a breathtaking tour-de-force.

— THAT GUY WHO'S ALWAYS AT STARBUCKS

A voice for a new generation.

— LONGTIME READER

Alex Lucas has truly exceptional taste in software.

— BEN REEDING

HOW TO TALK TO ANYONE ABOUT ANYTHING

FIND YOUR VOICE, OVERCOME SHYNESS AND GAIN SELF CONFIDENCE

ALEX LUCAS

CONTENTS

INTRODUCTION

Everyone has unique ways of expressing themselves. In my opinion, we all have a lot to say, but coming up with ways to say it is more than half the battle.

— Criss Jami, Salomé: In Every Inch In Every Mile

Have you ever experienced that feeling of being an outsider during a social gathering? You try to initiate a conversation, but it feels forced and awkward. While you long to break the unpleasant quiet, you also detest engaging in pointless small talk.

As an introvert, I've experienced this several times. I used to believe that making small talk was a necessary evil that I had to face to fit in. The truth is that small talk isn't the issue. The issue is that introverts prefer a more profound connection than the idle chitchat that often leads to people passing judgment on them rather than getting to know them. They detest treating others the same way.

Introverts yearn for meaningful conversations, which make us feel heard, valued, and understood. But getting those talks started can be difficult, particularly in social settings. We fear making a mistake, seeming foolish, or receiving criticism from others. As a result, we retreat into ourselves, altogether shunning social interactions or gritting our teeth through them.

However, the truth is that things don't have to be this way. Introverts can learn to enjoy social situations and flourish with the correct tools and techniques. This book fills that need.

So, this book is for you if you're an introvert who has trouble making small talk or an extrovert who wants to connect and understand introverts better. Let's practice having meaningful conversations and learning to talk to anyone about anything together.

The question now arises: how do you start conversations when you're an introvert? For many introverts, the social setting and communication challenges might be significant issues. Overcoming the anxiety of not knowing what to say, the fear of being judged, and the pressure to make a good impression can be challenging.

I am aware of the pain and frustration that introverts experience in these circumstances. As an introvert myself, I can attest to these difficulties. I wrote this book to share the knowledge and strategies I've acquired to help introverts like you overcome these challenges and take pleasure in meaningful interactions.

Maybe you've had trouble making friends, or perhaps you believe that your shyness or being too reserved prevents you from taking advantage of possibilities in your personal or professional life. Maybe you're sick of experiencing anxiety or feeling you're not being heard or understood in social settings.

Whatever your reason, I want you to know you're not alone. The same problems plague many introverts, but with the correct tools and techniques, you can get past them and engage in fulfilling interactions.

The information and expertise I'm sharing in this book are the results of years of practice, trial and error, reading, and attending seminars. I've helped introverts from all walks of life overcome their social phobias and enhance their social abilities.

These practical approaches have been tried in the most challenging social settings and have been effective.

Nevertheless, don't just take my word for it. Many other people, including famous people, influential businesspeople, and regular people from all walks of life, have succeeded in using the ideas and techniques I provide in this book.

Imagine entering a social gathering with ease and self-confidence, knowing you can start a conversation with anyone and carry it on. Imagine having meaningful interactions with others and feeling heard and understood. You will get these outcomes by reading this book and implementing the strategies.

It can be challenging to overcome social phobias and improve social skills, but it is doable. Developing conversational skills, engaging in more meaningful conversations, and establishing deeper connections with others is possible.

In the following pages, I'll share the knowledge and techniques that have helped me and many others become more assured and interesting conversationalists. You'll discover how to make the most of your introversion, make small talk count, and forge lasting relationships with others.

I can't wait to go on this adventure with you, and my goal is for you to come out of it with the ability and confidence to talk to anyone about anything. So, let's get going!

CHAPTER ONE

SOCIAL SKILLS YOU WISHED FOR

*M*ost of us experience social awkwardness, especially when we are about to be in the spotlight or interact with strangers. It's also widespread to feel shy, frightened, or uneasy in situations where we can be judged, such as an interview, meeting our partner's family, or beginning a new career.

This anxiety often passes with time and rarely prevents us from performing enjoyable and significant tasks. But, for some people, social anxiety can be crippling and negatively affect their quality of life, relationships, and employment. This is typically referred to as social anxiety.

If you often feel anxious about being judged by others or stressed out in social situations, you might benefit from learning more about social anxiety disorder.

WHAT IS SOCIAL ANXIETY?

People with social anxiety may experience crippling mental health problems that scare them in various social situations.

Social anxiety is a relatively common condition. Whether you or someone you know is exhibiting symptoms of social anxiety, you are not alone. According to estimates, 7% of adults in the US struggle with social anxiety.

Understanding social anxiety can help you manage symptoms and choose the best solution.

A social anxiety condition differs from the typical nervousness or butterflies one experiences in some social situations. Everyone has anxiety occasionally, whether it's a mild case of fear before going on a date or a case of anxiety before attending a significant event, job interview, or meeting. On the other hand, a social anxiety disorder can result in extremely high levels of stress, humiliation, or fear when attending social gatherings or going out in public.

If you suffer from a social anxiety disorder, you most certainly have an excessive fear of people scrutinizing or judging you in public settings.

Social anxiety disorder can manifest in a variety of social contexts. People may occasionally experience specific triggers, while others may suffer nonspecific, all-encompassing fear whenever they interact.

SIGNS AND SYMPTOMS OF SOCIAL ANXIETY

People often think social anxiety is just a feeling; however, social anxiety consists of four different factors: thoughts, feelings, physical sensations, and behaviors. Most people may first recognize their social anxiety when physical symptoms like trembling and crying are present, along with uneasiness. The four elements interact and reinforce one another when you're nervous, creating a vicious cycle of anxiety. For instance, here is how your anxiety can manifest if you're worried about giving a presentation at work:

- **Thoughts:** Anxiety often starts with a pessimistic idea, like "I'm going to mess up" or "People will think I'm stupid."
- **Emotions:** These thoughts make you experience unfavorable feelings like stress or fear.
- **Physical Sensation:** Your body responds negatively to your thoughts and feelings by sweating, blushing, or shivering.
- **Behaviors:** You may try to calm yourself down by doing something consciously or unconsciously, like avoiding eye contact or ducking behind the podium.

Your conduct may make you feel as though everyone is staring at you stiffly (anxious thinking), which can make you feel even more agitated) (an uneasy feeling).

People with social anxiety often don't recognize when their nervousness influences their behavior. Three types of behaviors are often seen in those who have social anxiety:

- **Avoidance behaviors:** Refraining from anxious-provoking circumstances. For instance, you might decline invitations to present at work.
- **Escaping behaviors:** When you leave situations that make you nervous, like a concert or party, after only a short while due to your anxiety.
- **Safety behaviors:** These are the steps you take to ease your social anxiety, such as drinking to relax or playing a game on your phone. In the above example, safety precautions include avoiding the presenter or hiding behind the podium.

WHY DO YOU HAVE SOCIAL ANXIETY?

Many different causes can contribute to the emergence of social anxiety. It might even date back to someone's childhood. Other people become anxious when something "triggers" them.

Remember, let's examine five reasons you may have social anxiety. You can start addressing social anxiety as soon as you better understand what's behind it.

1. Genetics

Anxiety problems can occasionally run in families and be inherited. You're 30–40% more likely to develop social anxiety disorder yourself if one or both of your parents struggled with it.

Some people with social anxiety disorder typically struggle to produce serotonin consistently. According to research, a particular gene that transports serotonin in the brain may be responsible for that.

Anxiety symptoms may result from the hormone being produced either in excess or insufficiently by this gene, which leads to brain instability.

2. Parental Approaches

Sometimes, social anxiety is caused by your parents' parenting style rather than your genes. There has been an investigation into the connection between social anxiety disorder and unfavorable parenting practices.

The results demonstrate that some parenting practices and parental characteristics can unquestionably cause anxiety in children.

For instance, criticizing or domineering parents may make their kids afraid of the outside world or of interacting with people and forming relationships.

A lack of warmth or compassion, rejection, and shame-based child training techniques are some parenting philosophies linked to the emergence of social anxiety.

You pick up things from your environment, including the fear of criticism from others. Hearing a parent's repeated expression of their fear of rejection by others is one environmental factor that might contribute to social anxiety. Even as adults, they could struggle to fit into social circles due to low self-esteem and lack of confidence.

3. Trauma

At any age, trauma can have long-lasting psychological effects. This may be particularly true if you endure a traumatic childhood event. In some circumstances, this might cause social anxiety as an adult.

You may have gone through trauma if you have been bullied, endured mental or physical abuse, witnessed domestic violence, or had a parent or other caregiver abandon you and your family.

These experiences teach you at a young age that life may be unpredictable and frightening.

You've learned that you may feel safer alone and won't damage yourself. However, those beliefs may prevent you from connecting with people who love you.

4. Handling grief

A loss in your life might also leave you unsure of many things. Social anxiety can be brought on by divorce, losing your job, or losing a loved one.

The first step in overcoming grief is recognizing your loss's truth. Individuals deal with grief in different ways. Your unwillingness to face the fact may be the root of your social anxiety.

You won't have to discuss your loss or acknowledge that it occurred if you don't go out into crowds of people. Because of this, some individuals tend to isolate themselves more often after losing a loved one.

5. Particular Triggers

The primary reason for social anxiety disorder isn't always apparent. Some people only exhibit symptoms in response to specific triggers.

Although each person's triggers are unique, some of the most typical ones are as follows:

- Going on a first date
- Speaking with superiors
- Meeting new people or groups of people

- Speaking in public
- Talking on the phone;
- Being watched while engaging in a new or unfamiliar activity
- Attending parties or events alone.

THE EFFECTS OF ANXIETY ON COMMUNICATION

Any form of anxiety has the potential to make it challenging to communicate. While some people may only experience the effects of their stress in social settings, others may experience constant symptoms.

When you have anxiety, there is no single problem that hinders communication. Instead, various potential problems could make communication challenging. Some examples include:

Distracted Thinking

Distracted thinking could be one of the main problems brought on by anxiety. You may worry about many things, obsess about your feelings, or become caught in one thought. Whatever the problem, distracted thinking makes it exceedingly difficult to listen and maintain a conversation, which impairs your capacity to communicate.

Overthinking Out of Anxiety

Overthinking might be problematic when you're anxious. To say the right thing, it's common to overthink every word you're about to say while speaking to someone when you're worried. But it disturbs the natural flow of communication if you constantly second-guess what you are about to say.

Verbal stuttering

Natural movements may seem strange or unnatural when anxiety is present. A good illustration is tripping over your tongue. Typically, your tongue makes the exact movements required to produce the desired sounds and letters. Yet, because your brain concentrates on that motion while you're anxious, it's common for some automatic body actions to become less intuitive. This could make it more difficult for your tongue to move naturally, which could cause you to stumble when speaking.

Headaches, confusion, and delusions of reality

Various factors might make it difficult to think clearly in some instances of intense anxiety, most notably with panic attacks. Your brain may get overloaded by stress. It can result in a loss of reality, which makes it difficult to hear or think clearly. Moreover, it may make you feel dizzy and impair your thinking. In these situations, the flawed thinking often doesn't get better until the panic attack has passed and your breathing has returned to normal.

Difficulty listening

Lastly, listening and understanding what the other person is saying can be challenging while you are preoccupied with your anxiety. This is often caused by the previously described distracted thinking and overthinking. Being overly preoccupied with a person's nonverbal cues or facial expressions can interfere with your ability to listen and focus on what they are saying. Anxiety about the content of the message may force you to concentrate too much on a single word or phrase, which may prevent you from hearing other important information that you need to listen to respond appropriately.

While anxiety can make it challenging to communicate, the type of anxiety you experience may cause you to encounter particular problems.

HOW TO COMBAT SOCIAL ANXIETY

Isolation can make a person depressed because it prevents you from having fun, enjoying yourself, and feeling connected to others. Even if it may be challenging, dealing with your social anxiety is crucial because it can significantly affect your life. It may have undetectable detrimental impacts on your job, friendships, love life, or even family ties. Lost opportunities may have a significant effect on you.

Although solutions for conquering social anxiety rely on your unique personality and how much the problem interferes with your life, it is a relatively treatable condition. A different form of treatment might be more effective for less severe anxiety. For instance, you might choose medicine, psychotherapy, or a mix of the two if you experience panic attacks when you go out in public because you feel overwhelmed.

Here are a few other strategies for overcoming social anxiety.

- Public speaking exercises
- Consider Cognitive Behavioral Therapy (CBT) as a treatment option.
- Slowly expose yourself to situations that make you anxious.
- Seek assistance from those who are there for you.
- Be honest with yourself.
- Look for the bright side and practice self-kindness.

TEN RULES THAT GOOD COMMUNICATORS FOLLOW TO BE CHARMING AND ENGAGING CONVERSATIONALISTS

Some people are born talkers who can engage anyone in conversation about anything. And for some people, small talk is difficult. Knowing what to talk about isn't what distinguishes the two; it's honing your communication skills so you can maintain a good conversation.

Maintaining a discussion requires a give and take as in a game of catch. If someone asks you a question, or if the ball is tossed your way, you should always answer in a way that will keep the conversation going by passing the ball back and never letting it drop.

When a musician is asked, "What kind of music do you play?" The answer "many different kinds" will end a conversation. It's essential to respond and elaborate. A better response to the same question could be, "I perform various kinds of music, although I spent my early twenties in the South playing a lot of country music, which I've subsequently applied to my music career in New York City." You can start a more exciting conversation by giving the other person something to work with.

Thoughts of conversation as a game of verbal tennis will keep the conversation moving, but mastering other communication techniques is necessary to become a successful conversationalist. The following are ten guidelines that will be discussed in the later chapters of this book:

1. Show sincere interest in the other person.
2. Pay attention to the positive.
3. Talk instead of dispute (or argue).
4. Respect.
5. Put the person in their best light.
6. Celebrate diversity while highlighting similarities.
7. Be true to who you are.
8. Sharing 50/50.
9. Ask meaningful questions.
10. Give and take.

THE 5 STAGES OF CONVERSATION

Conversational abilities are essential in daily life while presenting and in job interviews, though expectations may vary based on the field, degree, knowledge, and experience. An excellent conversationalist understands when to listen when to speak, and when to quit talking before the listeners tune out. Here, we categorize conversation into five stages, which we shall adapt here for our discussion.

1. Starting

During the beginning of a conversation, starting calls for your willingness to engage in conversation and may even entail the use of small talk to "break the ice." You may convey openness by using nonverbal cues like walking up to someone, stopping a few feet away, turning to face them, making eye contact, and smiling. For introverts, starting a conversation in new situations can be challenging.

2. Preview

The conversation topic is previewed verbally or nonverbally, as in, "Can I ask you how I can safely conduct this procedure?" Similar to emailing, a straightforward approach is usually good, although you might wish to preview a delicate subject indirectly. A boss might begin a conversation with a worker about arriving late to work too often by remarking, "That was some nightmare traffic on the highway this morning, eh?"

3. Business

You can now get straight to the point. Like establishing an agenda at a meeting, you can indicate to your conversation partner that you have three points to cover. This may come off as stiff at first, but if you pay attention to informal talks, you'll notice that there is often a natural, unspoken list of subtopics leading to a central point that keeps the conversation on track.

4. Feedbacks

Like the preview phase, this feedback allows speakers to elaborate on, reaffirm, or discuss the talking points to reach a consensus. In some cultures, the points and their response may repeat numerous times, or at the feedback stage, a simple "Are we good?" may suffice. Cross-cultural communication may require more time to establish a mutual understanding.

5. Closing

The shift to the conversation's conclusion is often signaled by accepting input from both parties. Closings are similar to the starting stage in that they can be communicated both orally (such as "All right, thanks! Bye") and nonverbally, such as by taking a step back and turning your body in the direction you're about to go to disengage while still facing and conversing with the other. When phrases like "Okay, one last thing" are used, the audience anticipates a conclusion and mentally moves on to the next topic. Mentioning a future meeting time, date, or location makes it apparent that the conversation will resume later, even though it is over.

More detail to come about mastering conversations in the succeeding chapters.

SOCIAL SITUATIONS AND YOU

You can use the ability to start a meaningful conversation to develop and strengthen relationships. You can speak with anyone, in any situation, by creating a list of conversation starters. You can use particular word selections to make a good first impression when you meet someone for the first time. This section explores 20 conversation starters and how to initiate a conversation with a stranger.

You can pick from different conversation starters in the workplace as long as they are appropriate. Conversation starters for new friends or acquaintances can differ from those for colleagues or business relations. Your early attempts spark a conversation that could lead to the development of valuable connections with coworkers and colleagues. Some of the finest approaches to striking up a conversation are as follows:

- Ask a question
- Give a compliment
- Talk about an event or situation
- Ask an opinion

- Offer help
- Ask for help
- Ask open-ended questions
- Share an interesting fact
- Make a useful comment
- Mention a mutual colleague
- Introduce yourself
- Ask for an update
- Talk about them
- Make an observation
- Discuss common interests
- Talk about a shared trait

Social situations which require learning how to start a great conversation with anyone include:

- Parties and dinners
- Family gatherings
- Weddings
- Funerals
- Meeting new people
- Speaking to someone experiencing grief
- Job offer

TRICKS UP YOUR SLEEVE

By starting a conversation, you've already taken a small step toward being a more successful communicator. You also need to maintain the conversation, which is often difficult due to anxiety because you might require some time to gather your thoughts and respond. In these circumstances, it is advantageous to have a repertoire of conversation-saving techniques that will allow you to appear as a polished conversationalist while you covertly take some time to consider your response.

Here are 17 tips to keep in mind as you get ready to respond to challenging questions intelligently and effectively:

1. Be ready for challenging questions

It might be good to anticipate questions you might be asked when getting ready for a crucial talk, interview, meeting, or presentation. Before the meeting, organize your ideas and potential responses to complex questions. Having a plan and knowing what to expect will help you feel less stressed.

2. Take a brief pause before answering

Take a moment to gather your thoughts before responding to a challenging question. This pause can offer you space to decide on an effective tactic, like humor, to handle the circumstance. You can prevent a reflexive reaction by taking a deep breath, gathering your ideas, and considering your response to the question.

3. Be aware of your nonverbal cues.

As you respond to challenging questions, pay attention to your tone, gestures, and facial expressions. Your nonverbal cues can carry just as much weight as your verbal ones. Be sure your body language supports the message you are trying to convey. For instance, your nonverbal clues would conflict with your words if you remark, "That's an interesting point," but are rolling your eyes or turning away. Here are ways to demonstrate that you are engaged in a conversation:

- Nod
- Establish eye contact
- Let your arms hang loose
- Take notes
- Shake hands at the end.

4. Rephrase the question

Be sure you fully comprehend what someone is asking you before answering a question. Think about rephrasing their question and returning the question by saying something like:

- "What you're asking is..."
- "In other words..."
- "From what I gather, you want to know..."

This gives you more time to gather ideas and helps you determine the original question. This extra step can assist you in deciding whether your solution addresses the person's genuine concern.

5. Take more time if you need it.

If you don't know the correct answer to a challenging question immediately, consider not responding directly. Instead of giving a quick but incorrect answer, take the time to gather pertinent information and make a complete, accurate response. In response, you can say:

- "Let me get back to you about that."
- "Before I can respond to that, I need to conduct some research."
- "Let me speak with [name/department] first because I don't want to give you the wrong information."

6. Respect the feelings of the other person

While answering a challenging question, be sensitive to the other person's feelings. They may feel more understood and seen as a result. Don't downplay their emotions. Instead, acknowledge their feelings and let them know you wish to deal with the problem causing their unpleasant feelings. You may respond with any of the following:

- "I understand that you're upset; I can see it."
- "This situation frustrates me as well."
- "That does sound challenging."

7. Address a portion of the question.

Identify a section of a challenging topic you can respond to now. You might concentrate on a question's less contentious or emotive component. You could propose setting up a second meeting to go over more issues. Consider saying, "Let's address this for the time being…."

8. Ask more questions about the question

Occasionally, someone asks a difficult question due to a deeper problem. Understanding this person's viewpoint and intentions is vital before starting a contentious conversation. You can use the following questions to learn more about someone's perspective and motivations:

- Why are you asking?
- Why does that matter so much to you?
- Why do you feel that way, exactly?
- What informs your viewpoint on that subject?
- Why do you need to know the answer?
- Do you have any prior knowledge in this area?

9. Ask the asker to define any unclear term.

Consider asking someone to clarify their meaning in their own words when they ask you a question. This is particularly useful for defusing unclear or contentious terminology and preventing misunderstandings. You want to know exactly what the other person is thinking before you respond so that your reaction is pertinent and suitable. Here are a few strategies for handling confusing terms:

- "What do you mean specifically by [word]?"
- "What makes this situation feel [word] to you?"
- "How are you defining [word] in this context?"

10. Transition to a different topic

Consider bridging when facing a difficult question you don't want to respond to. Bridging is moving from a challenging question to a topic you want to discuss. Say something like, "That reminds me of..." It's a polite technique to turn the subject of the discussion or the presentation away from a pointless or baited question.

11. Funneling to the topic you want to discuss

You can funnel the conversation, which is similar to bridging. Funneling means starting with broad questions and working toward narrowing your focus. This can help you determine the specific nature of the other person's worry. The open-ended questions help to start the conversation and get people talking. You can discover the person's particular concerns or frustrations as the questions get more focus.

Consider these series of questions for a funneling example:

- What aspect of your profession do you enjoy the most?
- What characteristics do you value most in a coworker?

- Have you ever been in a heated argument with a coworker?
- How do you handle disagreements at work?

12. Let the other person lead the discussion.

Instead of taking charge during a challenging conversation, think about letting the other person guide your response. This may allow them to focus on themselves and deal with their emotions if they are anxious or upset rather than projecting them outward. You might say:

- How would you like me to handle this?
- Do you want me to share this information with you?
- What result do you expect to get out of this?

13. Exercise decency and respect.

Be kind while answering challenging questions. Being approachable and friendly might help calm a tense situation. It's crucial to behave professionally and politely while you're at a meeting or presentation with other people because doing so might encourage them to do the same.

14. Steer clear of emotional responses

It might be tricky to stay composed when responding to complex questions. You want to demonstrate that you can maintain composure and focus in high-pressure circumstances since your response reflects your character. Here are some methods for responding in a way that restrains your emotional reaction when you're feeling challenged:

- Short answers are preferable
- Respond specifically to the question and avoid tangents
- Facts should be used to back up your response
- Moving quickly to the next question would be best to refocus your attention.

15. Make the other person feel at ease

Make an effort to relate to the individual who is questioning you. Please find a way to connect their question with pertinent information and let them know that you value their inquiry.

Think of a meeting where you're introducing a new piece of software to the staff. A frustrated person can ask how long it takes to learn this new program. You may say, "I know learning a new program can be overwhelming, but we have planned in-depth training sessions. We are convinced that once you master this program, your job will be much more fun because it allays many of the department's worries with the present program. Your productivity, workflow, and communication will all be enhanced."

16. Use humor

A lighthearted remark during a complex argument can help to calm things down. In a meeting or presentation, humor can help everyone unwind and reset by reducing the tension that could come with a difficult question.

17. Take a break when necessary

It could be wise to stop talking if you think the other person deliberately tries to make you uncomfortable or is looking for a challenge. Here are some suggestions about how to end a conversation professionally and politely:

- "I'd rather not talk about this at the moment."
- "That topic is too complex for discussion right now."
- "Why don't we switch to a different topic?"

Nonverbal communication is among the numerous tools available to help you come across favorably in interviews and your professional life. However, it is essential to state that hiring decisions should be made based on a candidate's skills and credentials. Businesses should endeavor to be diverse and accept everyone's unique communication preferences.

WORKSHEET

Write down some small sentences you can use when you need a minute to think and rearrange your scrambled thoughts. These will help you overcome your anxiety, and then you can respond in social situations.

For example:

- Uh, let me think
- Okay, so you mean to say…. (repeat what they said to confirm you heard them right, it also helps in discerning the meaning)
- Yeah, let me see how I can help you with this
- Hmm… good question
- I'll see what I can do for you
- Oh, I see

1. ....

2. ....

3. ....

4. ....

5. ....

6. ....

7. ....

8. ....

9. ....

10. ....

CHAPTER TWO

SETTING YOUR INTENTIONS STRAIGHT

*O*ur conversations will become easier to navigate when we have a clear intention. To initiate a conversation without a purpose is like going into the desert without a compass. Yet despite not having one, we often engage in discussions without even a hazy notion of how we want the conversation to go. Instead of being clear about what we want, whether to establish our truth, exchange perspectives, deepen our understanding, learn about another person's life, or practice listening, we go in blind and end up stumbling all over the place. We lose ourselves in complex, subliminal motivations ranging from the desire to be correct and disprove others to the desire to display our superior knowledge and assert our control. We get caught up in trying to win over others or to defend ourselves. When feelings arise, we don't know how to deal with them; instead, we ignore them or find other ways to get by, like wading across unforeseen stretches of desert or soggy swamps. Our meaningful interactions often get dragged out, aimless, disappointing, and tiresome.

The main point of this chapter is to talk about the intentions behind each interaction that the readers will have. We will elaborate on how the right intent behind a conversation always helps people push aside their biases and indulge in deeper, honest discussions.

INTENT VS. IMPACT

Have you ever intended for things to go one way but ended up with something entirely different? It might be challenging to balance an action's intent with its impact.

You had good intentions. You intended to change something at work, but the outcome hurt your team.

When confronted with what transpired, all you can say is, "But that's not what I meant to happen!"

That is impact vs. intent. These are different, and failing to recognize this difference can result in disagreement. When you approach a conversation with intention, the other person cannot read your mind. However, they'll see the impact of your actions.

As a result, your intent doesn't convert into your intended impact. Let's talk about effects vs. intent and how you may consider both to promote honest and open communication.

The main difference between impact and intent

The saying "The road to hell is paved with good intentions" indicates that even when excellent intentions are made, the impacts may still be damaging. Often, your purpose and the effect you have are different. This is why:

1. Your intent is what you have in mind, while the impact is what happens in reality.

To understand this difference further, let's examine the definitions of intent and impact.

- What does "intent" mean? The intent is what you have in mind as a goal when you choose to act. It indicates the kind of impact you hope your actions will have.
- What does "Impact" mean" Impact is the outcome of those acts. The impact of your actions reflects their reality. However, the results may only be what you had in mind.

2. Impact, instead of intent, refers to how your actions make others feel.

When you execute an action, you feel a specific way about it. Your intention and how you think are related.

Yet, the impact relates to how your action affects the receiver's feelings. Even if you initially feel fantastic about your intentions, the recipient will still be upset.

3. Impact is what you did, while the intent is who you are your personality and intentions are related; therefore, having good intentions may indicate that you genuinely want to help others.

It may indicate that you are helpful if you wish to help someone. If you're willing to try something new at work, it may suggest that you're imaginative and receptive.

Failure due to your influence does not imply that you are a failure. It doesn't accurately represent who you are. Yet what you did had an impact.

What's more, remember this difference when someone tells you how your actions impacted them. They are not criticizing you personally if they claim your actions hurt them.

Instead of taking it personally, try to understand how your actions impacted them while you listen.

Understanding when someone has good intentions

First, remember that your ideas and feelings are entirely under your control. You have absolute control over how you perceive a situation. Consider some things if someone else's good intentions negatively impact you.

It would be best to ask about the other person's intentions. Letting them explain their intent can help put what happened in perspective.

You'll be able to tell whether or not they had sincere intentions. But this doesn't take away from their impact. You can express your feelings without blaming them for how their actions made you feel.

Here's an illustration:

"I understand you intended to improve this project, but I'm anxious about what transpired." This sentence declares the intention. But it also illustrates the impact.

What it's like to be impacted

Even when you mean well, it's essential to understand what it's like to be impacted by your actions. You have no power over someone else's emotions. Only your intentions and actions are under your control. You are unable to undo a decision after you have made it.

All you can do at this point is acknowledge how the other person feels due to your actions. If the other person feels wounded or offended, don't dismiss their feelings. It doesn't matter, even if you didn't want them to feel this way. The reality is that they do.

Express regret for the outcome of your actions. Ensure your apology is genuine and doesn't place the onus of responsibility on the victim. Here is an illustration of what not to say:

"I'm sorry if what I did caused you to stress.

This denies that the other person was harmed and instead places the blame on them. Using the word "if" assumes the possibility that they might have been hurt.

Here's a more effective apology: "I'm sorry that my actions caused you to stress."

The phrase "My actions caused" shows that this statement accepts responsibility for the consequences. That is clearer than stating "if," which conveys uncertainty and may lead to mistrust.

There is no "if" in the other person's feelings because they informed you how they felt. As a result, you can converse transparently, honestly, and straightforwardly.

PURPOSE OF CONVERSATION

Discussing new concepts, reviewing old ones, and inciting vigorous discussion are always beneficial. Hence, things remain fascinating. Also, talking is beneficial for our well-being. Here are a few explanations why even the most introverted person should occasionally find a conversation partner.

Good stuff comes in small packages.

Even small talk is beneficial to your health. According to a 2010 University of Michigan study, socializing with coworkers while working in the kitchen can similarly enhance cognitive abilities as brain-teaser exercises.

We become better problem solvers through small talk. So, conversing with Bobby from marketing about your weekend or telling Susan in accounts about the lovely weather could be just as productive as solving a crossword puzzle.

We are fallible

We better grasp topics and issues that we might otherwise take for granted by being open to the conversation of new ideas and viewpoints, including those we disagree with.

We are only sometimes going to get things right. Conversations help us remember this. Knowledge shared through chat could influence our points of view or validate our original perspective.

Social support

You get social support by talking to people. Whether you chat with your friends, coworkers, and family members to share information, get advice, or vent, doing so will help you put things in perspective, which will help you develop resilience and handle setbacks better.

EXPLAINING YOUR INTENT

When we engage in conversations, the majority of us rarely, if ever

- State our intentions or goals for the exchanges, even for ourselves
- Even less often, explain our choices or plans for the discussion to the other party.

This is unfortunate because having clear intentions and being able to explain them to others can improve communication and understanding.

Start essential conversations by encouraging your conversation partner to join you in the specific conversation you want to have to increase cooperation and minimize potential misunderstandings. The more critical the discussion will be to you, the more crucial for your conversation partner to understand the big picture. Suppose you must conduct a lengthy, intricate, or emotionally charged conversation with someone. In that case, it will significantly impact if you briefly describe your conversational intention before asking for your intended conversation partner's approval.

Many effective communicators do this automatically when stating intentions or asking for consent. They introduce themselves and begin conversations with phrases like:

- "Hello, Steve. I need your assistance with my assignment. Have a minute to discuss it?

- "Jane, do you have a moment?" I want to discuss something with you right now. Is that okay?
- "Well, sit down for a moment and allow me to explain what transpired..."
- "Good day, Mr. Julius. I'm uncomfortable with this job. Let's discuss it.
- "Hello, Jerry. I'm Mike. How are you? I want to discuss Fred with you. He's back behind bars. Is it a good time to talk now?

As you can see, each of the examples has two components. First, the declaration of intent explains what the speaker intends to discuss and provides some justification. The second entails requesting the other person's permission.

Here are four crucial ways that such coupled explanations of intent and invites to consent might advance our conversations:

- First, we provide our listeners the option of accepting or rejecting the offer of a particular conversation. Participation will be more active for someone who has consented to take part.
- Second, we help our listeners understand the "big picture," or the ultimate objective of the conversation that will follow. (Many linguists and communication researchers now concur that understanding a person's overall conversational intent is essential for

deciphering their message through words and body language.)

- Third, we give our listeners time to prepare for what is to come, especially if the topic is sensitive. (If we start emotional conversations unexpectedly with individuals, they might react by avoiding us in the future or being on guard all the time.)
- Fourth, we explain to our listeners what part they should play in the dialogue, such as a fellow problem solver, an employee receiving instructions, a provider of emotional support, etc. These are incredibly different roles to perform. If we only ask others to participate in one conversational part at a time, our conversations flow more smoothly.

YOUR INTENTION IS WHERE YOU MIGHT GO WRONG IN A CONVERSATION

When conversations don't go as intended, or when someone misunderstands us, it can be unnerving and unpleasant and produce unnecessary conflict or hurt emotions at home or in the workplace.

Some things can go wrong when we are speaking with one another. Examples include the rhythms, intonation patterns, how quickly you get to the point, and humor.

There are some essential suggestions to help you communicate better with others. Here they are:

The first step is to be aware of your and other people's conversational styles. Think about things like communication styles that you prefer—direct or indirect—the duration of pauses, or if talking with someone will be seen as a show of excitement or, on the other hand, an unwelcome interruption. To avoid coming out as impolite, you should aim for a shared conversational or speaking style.

A direct response is a yes or no. While it is indirect to respond with your question, such as "What do you wish to do?" To illustrate the difference between direct and indirect communication, consider the following example: Would you like to stop for a drink?

This is important because, despite the unique benefits of direct and indirect speech, differences in choice might result in serious misunderstandings. This typically arises when one person has a predetermined notion of how the other would respond. For instance, if I anticipate a direct response, the ambiguity of an indirect response may confuse or irritate me.

There may also be cultural variances in how an indirect reply is interpreted. This is an example of a woman discussing his desire to attend a party with her Greek husband. She assumed her husband didn't want to participate in the party because he responded indirectly, but the opposite was true. Then she researched how people in Greece would react to his response.

Finally, remember to take both the message and the meta-message into account. The news is the word's meaning, while what it says about the relationship is the meta-message.

What, for instance, did our conversation disclose about our position to each other? Did it place one person higher and one lower? Did it widen or narrow our distance?

When we disagree in conversation, it's often not what was said that makes us angry; instead, it's the impact those comments will have on our relationship.

HOW INTENTIONS CONTROL CONVERSATIONS AND IMPACT YOUR LIFE

Half the battle is won with good planning. That also applies to the conversation you have. If you have a solid understanding of the other party and decide on a specific aim before you begin, you may have a better-organized meeting where your influence will be more decisive. Still, the conversation can take a different route. There is no pause button to press, which is one of the reasons as well as the fact that you can never predict what someone else will say or do! However, your subconscious thinking also has an impact.

Are you creating or preventing?

90% of our actions are the result of unconscious internal processes. Our thoughts, emotions, and presumptions greatly influence our attitudes about a scenario. We have already established an intention based on these before beginning a conversation: we either wish to generate or prevent something. Your goal in initiating this conversation might be to "avoid the client getting upset," as this often results in feelings of fear or resistance. For instance, you have worked longer than anticipated. One possibility is that the client won't agree or pay for the extra hours.

Your thoughts will manifest as your truth.

This kind of intention will significantly influence how you conduct the conversation. It even affects the physical processes in your body. You'll feel agitated (cortisol levels will rise), and your muscles will tense up when you have a bad intention. Your thoughts will come true; thus, the psychological impact will be even more significant. According to research, you always do worse when you believe you can't accomplish something. The good news is that it also works the other way around. You'll do better if you start thinking and accepting that you can do it.

What presumptions do you, therefore, bring to a conversation? Let these go by addressing them in an open, sincere, and enquiring approach and determining whether they are true. You'll notice a more relaxed tone of voice inside yourself, keeping you in control and leading to a better result! Set a good intention after that.

ESTABLISHING THE PROPER INTENTIONS

Establishing conversational intents differs from having a goal and guiding the conversation toward it. The discussions must naturally flow and remain unbound by a particular destination.

Why is this conversation meaningful? What should be explored? How might a conversation shed light on this from fresh angles?

Don't Have a Goal

When we have a plan for where we want a venture to go, it usually goes more smoothly. Clear targets are easier to reach. Our culture has embraced goals and objectives. As Walt Disney's brother said about his success, "Because he could see it, we can all now see it."

However, should a conversation have a predetermined goal? A dialogue must be open to whatever comes up if it is to be genuine. We end up with a presentation, or worse, manipulation, if one has a predetermined outcome. Nevertheless, tangential conversations that end up nowhere can deflate our enthusiasm.

Establish an intention

It is preferable to have clear intentions in conversation rather than rigid goals. Clear choices entail choosing a course but not a destination. Purposes enable exploration that could find things that are better and different than what is anticipated. This search extends beyond seeking out answer X. Search, and ye shall find, but beware of being overly preoccupied with your theory or excessively minor detail.

When conversations are unexpected, challenging, and fresh, they become fantastic.

ADDING VALUE TO OTHER PERSON'S LIFE THROUGH CONVERSATIONS

Having a natural gift of gab is okay to be a great communicator. Just like emotional intelligence, this can also be learned. It simply requires effort, commitment, and self-awareness. If you want to improve your communication skill and increase professional success, you should think about mastering the following eight things:

1. Be real

People have the same sense of smell as dogs. We usually feel anxious, especially when speaking to influential people or sizable groups. The conversations where people admit to feeling uneasy or not quite themselves are occasionally the most energizing because they expose our vulnerability. What is unacceptable is when we overcompensate by putting on airs, claiming to be someone we are not, or changing our manner. Don't try to be someone you're not; genuine individuals are unforgettable.

2. Connect on a personal level

Make the recipient of your message feel as though it matters. Most of us only pay attention to what is being said if it connects with us on a deeper level. Discover that personal link, then tap on it. Please find a way to bring up that shared interest, whether you both have children, are from the same city, or have similar beliefs. It will improve the quality of your connection and the significance of what you're saying.

3. Be succinct, straightforward, and specific.

Effective communicators say what they want to say swiftly, precisely, and briefly. People's attention spans today are minute at most (if we're lucky), and they get lost in long sentences and significant words. Choose basic, straightforward messaging and cut right to the chase.

4. Listen with empathy

Everyone desires to be heard. Both recognition and visibility are something we seek. Active listening is one of many approaches to accomplish this. It involves doing something that only 2% of people do. Please add the reference. Empathic acknowledgment is the term for it. This is the ability to hear what is said without offering advice or linking it to you. All you need to do is acknowledge the person's feelings and tell them you have listened. Saying something as simple as, "I can understand how sad this makes you," is often more effective than trying to address the issue. It's been stated that if you can pull this off, the other person will feel like they have received a psychological hug. It's challenging, but you'll stand out and make the other person feel fantastic if you succeed.

5. Ask Questions

There's nothing worse than finishing a conversation and learning that the person didn't ask a single question, but it still happens often. When we ask how the other is doing, we show the other person that we care about them and make an informal environment. To succeed, you must pay attention to the responses and avoid daydreaming.

6. Recognize nonverbal cues

You can better serve your audience's demands when you can recognize signals and interpret your audience. For instance, if you're giving a presentation and some of the audience members have their arms crossed over their chests, they're probably not listening to what you're saying (unless it's freezing outside, in which case you might want to turn off the air conditioning). Whether on purpose or not, crossing our arms impacts how receptive we are to the conversation. Hence, the objective would be to move them and uncross their arms in this circumstance. You can ask the individual to make notes on the board, offer them a drink of water, hand them a marker, or get them to stand up. Make a move that will compel them to change their position. You can change your speech to maximum influence if you understand body language.

7. Communicate positively by switching the word "but to and."

Most people need to be aware of how our interactions can be significantly impacted by the words we use or how we communicate. How and what we say affects the flow of our interactions. For instance, when we use the word "but" in a sentence, everything that has come before is immediately deleted. It's terrible as so many amazing things are expressed before the 'but'; however, as humans, we focus primarily on the 'post-but' information.

- I adore your blog; it's funny and educational but could be more practical. Try using "and" instead of "but" when making a statement. Use these two phrases as an illustration:
- I appreciate your blog; it's funny and educational, and making it a little more practical would increase its impact.

Do you see a difference?

Not only does this make you reevaluate the message you want to portray, but it also changes your tone and gives each statement equal weight.

8. Think first, then speak

A rule says I always put off communicating through email, phone, text, or in person until the next day if I'm having a poor day, haven't had enough sleep, or am just in a "mood." I choose to remain silent 50% of the time. I'm still on board with what I want to communicate the next day. Giving anything some thought, you allow time to consider if you wish to convey that message. It helps us avoid impulsive responses, organize our ideas, and communicate our message as effectively as possible.

WORKSHEET

Introduce your conversational intent to get your conversation partner to pay attention. Describe the type of conversation you would like to have. Start by saying, "Right now, I'd want to...," or, "I'd like to take around 1/5-7/30 minutes and..." Try starting each of the conversations on the list with your practice partner—note which seems more straightforward, to begin with, and which seems more difficult.

An Experimental List of Conversational Intentions That Work

"I'd like to take a few minutes right now and..."

1. ... talk to you about my feelings/experience……
   without making any overt demands or complaints to

you OR …so you will understand the request, offer, complaint, etc., I want to make.

2. …listen to what's going on with you. (More precisely: hear how you are doing with [topic].

3. …tell you a story to amuse you.

4. …look at some potential options for.. (requiring your empathy but not your advice or permission)

5. …develop a plan of action for myself (with your assistance or just as a listener/witness).

6. …coordinate/plan our actions concerning…

7. …confess my love for you (or my gratitude to you for…)

8. …show my concern for you while you navigate a challenging circumstance.

9. …make a request or complain about something you did (or said) (for better resolution of conflicts, translate complaints into requests)

10. … confirm that I understand the experience or viewpoint you just described. (This is often followed by 'Sounds like you…', 'I hear that you…', 'Let me see if I understand you…' or 'So you're feeling kind of…')

11. …put an end to a disagreement I have with you concerning…

12. …bargain or haggle with you over…

13. …help you in deciding on…

14. …obtain your permission or consent to… /…grant you permission or consent to…

15. …give you some information about… /…ask you for information about…

16. …give you some suggestions about… / seek your opinion on…

17. …give you instructions, commands, or tasks… /… receive instructions or orders from you

18. …ask something of you (for time, action, information, money, object, promise, etc.)

19. …accept (or reject) a request you have made of me.

20. …make you an offer (for information, action, object, promise, etc.)

21. …accept or reject your offer.

22. …influence or inspire you to embrace (a specific) point of view.

23. …persuade or inspire you to take (a specific) course of action.

24. beg your pardon for… /…forgive you for…

25. …make an apology to you regarding… / ask you to apologize about…

26. …ask for your interpretation of… / offer an interpretation of…

27. … assess of… (how good or awful I think… is) / request your assessment of…

28. …change the conversation and talk about…

29. …take some time to consider your options.

30. …leave/stop this conversation so I can…

Your notes on this exercise

....

....

....

....

....

....

....

....

....

....

....

Exercise

Before starting a conversation the next time, take a moment to compose your intention. Think about that intention again at various moments throughout the conversation and let it shape your contribution. Consider whether your experience was affected by having a clear choice.

The next chapter helps develop meaningful relationships, which is a valuable skill to becoming a conversation expert.

CHAPTER THREE

A PINCH OF MEANING

We all understand the value of meaningful conversations, but we must consider why they are essential to our relationships. Our daily lives are significantly influenced by human connection, and relationships give us a sense of joy that nothing else appears to be able to match. They are essential for development, growth, and general well-being. Maintaining good connections—relationships that encourage rather than dissuade, relationships that are enduring rather than transitory—is significantly impacted by meaningful conversations. Our connections can start to wither if we don't have meaningful conversations. The more they fade, the more likely these relationships will be harmed and eventually fall apart. I've discovered that there is a more profound significance to practically everything we do and say daily. And if we don't have these in-depth conversations, we won't fully understand the intentions behind other people's acts. Adopting these mindful relationship practices will enable us to create solid foundations for all future relationships.

I'll use one example as an illustration. Consider a friend of yours who struggles with anxiety. Each person experiences anxiety uniquely, but it always leads to a shift in behavior. Some people become more reserved and silent, while others get angrier or more depressed. You might never understand what your friend is going through if you don't have these deep, meaningful conversations with them. You may experience misunderstandings, anger, resentment, and increased anxiety because you are unsure of your friend's reasons for doing that. Your relationship could suffer as a result of this. However, this situation would have encouraged a more robust connection than distance if you had already entered the relationship with mindful relationship skills.

The main point of this chapter is to help you make meaningful conversation with anyone.

People are great at assuming. Also, since individuals tend to withdraw when in pain, the situation becomes lethal. When we don't have all the facts, we often make assumptions and place blame. We think, why are they upset with me? Why are they not speaking with me? Did I make a mistake? Regular thoughtful, meaningful interactions help us develop connections that promote openness and enable us to ask for advice and assistance when needed.

COMMUNICATING WITHOUT ANY FORM OF MANIPULATION

Many "communication pros" do not distinguish between communication and manipulation. Fear and seduction are two methods of manipulation. Honest communication is achieved through genuinely understanding other people's goals, concerns, and situations. The difference is significant for both moral and pragmatic reasons.

Manipulation differentiates between relationships and outcomes because, if I choose manipulation, I will sacrifice relationships to achieve my goals. I give up on sincere cooperation out of a narrow-minded desire for gain. The connection is broken, and ultimately people will realize this. Even if it takes some time to learn the lie, we can all recognize when we have been manipulated. So why all the manipulation, then? Ignorance, hopelessness, and incompetence are what I am currently thinking. Few people know the costs of manipulation and the rewards of genuine connection; the memory of previous failed relationships (personal and professional) lowers confidence; ignorance and hopelessness stifle our natural desire to excel at establishing and maintaining valuable relationships. The cost is high because trust, imagination, resiliency, and practical action are products of genuine relationships. The results of manipulation cannot compare to those of open relationships.

HOW TO COMMUNICATE WITHOUT MANIPULATING PEOPLE

I've encountered my fair share of manipulative people. Some politicians regard public policy as a performance, much like professional wrestlers. People have given powerful speeches on stage before getting down and expressing their utter disagreement with what they had said (in private). Regardless of whichever side of the aisle you're on, there is no denying that manipulative people are on both sides.

Not only is manipulating people morally wrong, but eventually, they figure out what is happening. Lying and manipulating people will only work in the short run; thus, there are better long-term approaches than lying.

I've considered how similar the characteristics of all the manipulative persons I've seen over the years are. Even though this is not a comprehensive list, it is intriguing that manipulators follow a similar pattern.

Here are some characteristics that manipulators have in common:

- They often use partial truths. They combine half-truths with reality and conveniently leave out key elements to sell their position. As most manipulators are savvy with words, bringing them to justice in a court of law would be challenging.

- Severe need for boundaries. Those who are "master manipulators," in my opinion, lack moral boundaries and will say and do everything to craft their messages.
- Employ guilt as a weapon. One of the most potent causes driving manipulation is guilt. Unfortunately, many people use "guilt trips" to control other people.

Knowing these characteristics will help you recognize when someone purposely tries to manipulate you.

I urge you to inspire others around you rather than trying to control them! Here are some suggestions to get people to support your ideas:

- Being honest is the best policy. To communicate persuasively, you DO NOT need to fabricate details and tell lies. You increase your chances of forming a genuine connection with someone by being sincere and open with them.
- Put an end to the "blame game." Blaming others is rarely considered a positive leadership trait. Most people despise it when they hear someone blaming someone else for their failures. Instead, accept accountability for your deeds.
- Steer clear of passive-aggressive actions. Unfortunately, many individuals try to be

manipulative when persuading others to do what they want. They seek passive-aggressive methods to control others rather than using their stories to inspire others. This behavior does not foster trust, is improper, and does not motivate others to take action.

I implore you to overcome any manipulative tendencies you may have. Focus on inspiration rather than manipulation. People don't want to be used; they want to be inspired and uplifted.

6 WAYS YOU'RE MANIPULATING OTHERS WITHOUT EVEN REALIZING IT

Virtually everyone has experienced manipulation at some point in their lives, but nobody wants to believe that they are manipulative themselves. However, some actions are so frequent that you can use emotional coercion without awareness. In essence, manipulative behavior is "communicating in a circuitous way," It can manifest itself in various ways, from the silent treatment to more subtle actions. It persuades someone to act or think without addressing it directly.

The issue is that indirect communication can lead to problems in all kinds of personal relationships, including those with your family, significant other(s), coworkers, and friends. The recipient may be forced to do things they don't want to through habitual manipulative behavior because it makes it difficult for them to say no. This might develop resentment over time. Irritation develops when this happens regularly.

Here are some terrible behaviors you might have and better-coping mechanisms to help you maintain harmony in your relationships.

1. However, wouldn't you like...?

"Innocent" suggestion," when someone proposes something instead of genuinely articulating what they're feeling or thinking," is one example of manipulative behavior. For instance, if you text a friend while driving to their house and ask, "Don't you want some wine? I'll pick up a bottle," even though you're aware that your friend is not a big fan, the truth is that you could certainly use a glass or two. A more direct way to express your desire to say, "I think I want some wine with dinner; would you be interested?" Instead of trying to make your idea or desire look like someone else's. The tactic at work is to make it seem like theirs.

2. Entirely up to you, but...

Giving someone a choice when you already know what you want is similar to behavior. For instance, asking a friend which of two movies they'd prefer to see, then pointing out why one choice is preferable but still letting them keep their choice. This false-choice scenario might be phrased as "I'm entirely open—but this movie is far more historical, and we could certainly learn a lot."

It is coercive to present something as a choice when your goal is to steer someone toward a particular course of action. Being upfront about your preferences is a more direct way to ask the same question: "I'm leaning toward this movie. What do you think?

3. I forgot again (and again).

You wouldn't be alone if you've ever "forgotten" to complete a shared responsibility like a household chore because it was late, you were exhausted, or you didn't feel like it.

However, you should have a look at yourself if you often leave your partner or roommates to do the dishes or pick up the slack on team tasks. It is unfair to ignore matters that concern everyone consistently; if you are genuinely too exhausted or overburdened, you should discuss it. It is preferable to be open and honest when discussing what has to be done and possible solutions.

4. Make more promises

Another action that might be manipulative is overpromising. This could take the form of exaggerating how unique an event you want a friend to attend will be ("It'll be amazing! Tyra Banks is on the guest list!") or making a promise but not keeping it ("I'll make dinner every night this week!"). The other person is likely to be upset or furious when you don't live up to your half of the bargain after you've raised expectations, and they might even feel manipulated. Be straightforward, and if your friend or partner declines to do something, sincerely ask why. Most importantly, don't try to coerce someone into doing what you want; instead, only ask why.

5. I'll do it myself...

Even if it's harmful, playing the martyr can persuade people to comply with your wishes. It is futile to request help when you need it if you pressure someone in an indirect manner that could lead to guilt. It is manipulative to phrase your wants in a way that implies a negative outcome, but it doesn't matter if you do or don't do it. Make sure your request is as fair and reasonable as possible (for example, did you give the person you are asking enough notice?), then be honest about what you require.

6. Silent treatment

Unbelievably, staying silent can also exert emotional pressure. When you avoid discussing a problem or simply a feeling of injustice, you leave the other person with little choice except to make an effort to make you happy.

'Breaking them down' into an apology is a common practice. It's acceptable to take some time to relax, but if the break is too long, the other person may feel pressured to submit.

Ironically, this behavior often results from a place of hurt. When someone uses silence as a weapon, they are unintentionally being manipulative. That is a futile method of coping with the pain. It's always best to set the record straight so that your friend or partner may explain their actions without feeling pressured to offer an apology that they may not believe is warranted and could cause animosity in the future.

SO, WHAT ARE MEANINGFUL RELATIONSHIPS?

Meaningful relationships feature mutual respect, trust, interest, favorable regard, and making the other person feel appreciated. Building on these relationships is crucial since doing so will help you feel less lonely and reduce the symptoms of depression and anxiety. Building on principles of honesty and identifying commonalities will help lay the groundwork for these relationships to flourish.

By fostering a more profound connection, relationships give people a sense of purpose and belonging. The experience of being seen and respected, an improved mood and feeling of self-worth, the ability to express oneself, the development of support, and the production of brain chemicals like dopamine and endorphins are just a few advantages of long-lasting relationships. Sadly, it might be challenging to maintain these relationships in person because people tend to get preoccupied with their life affairs. Using virtual platforms, attentive listening, and reaching out to friends, you can further develop your relationships and improve your communication.

People often overlook some of the ways they can improve their relationships, but the following simple routines can help you and your relationships in more ways:

- **Reach out.** When we discover someone hasn't talked to us for a while, we can feel frustrated since we can sometimes get caught up in our worlds but try to remember that they might be experiencing something similar. Take the initiative by making contact with them.
- **Interact online.** Technology can be a terrific tool for staying in touch when life becomes hectic, thanks to online services like FaceTime, Zoom, Skype, and even group text messages! The upside to technology is regular, casual connection.
- **Honor boundaries.** There are limitations to what one individual can provide us. Try to appreciate that some individuals, especially those struggling, require time for sleep, work, family, and space.
- **Active listening.** Spend some time in your relationships being genuinely present. Respect them and express interest in them. Please take note of what they are saying or experiencing. Please make an effort to support them by asking them questions.

Consider who might be there to support you in times of need. Remember that you are never alone, and everyone has something to contribute. It may be time to speak with a mental health expert if you have trouble forming relationships with others. They can help you in locating those in your life who are supportive.

IMPORTANCE OF MEANINGFUL CONNECTIONS

An interpersonal relationship is the foundation of the human experience. We develop and improve when we have a small group of people we trust to impart wisdom. Beyond our physical and emotional well-being, we can thrive in fulfilling relationships with others.

Instilling this way of thinking in our children at a young age is one of the difficulties of parenting. This makes it more likely that when they are in their teen and early adult years, they will have developed a reliable network that will lift them rather than hold them behind. In other words, we should teach our children that actively seeking relationships with older people who exhibit these qualities is acceptable—even wise—in addition to teaching them how to recognize trustworthiness, wisdom, honesty, and integrity in those in their peer networks. On a related point, it's critical that once found, these individuals are willing participants in the process and are capable of pouring into others constructively and healthily.

Taping into such a network is a powerful personal and spiritual development tool. The advantages also work both ways. Your trusted network has much to give you, and they can gain knowledge from your experiences. This applies to both our children and us as parents.

Naturally, there are more justifications for meaningful relationships than just these three. However, for this book, here are the top three benefits of having meaningful relationships in our lives:

Validation

Life is a teacher. If we pay attention, every scenario and experience that comes our way has something to give. Yet when we tell those closest to us about our experiences, they often lend support or highlight the lessons that should be drawn from them.

Revelation

Getting perspective on where we are in life can be challenging. A good friend may provide much-needed clarity to our life, whether it's because we've overcommitted ourselves to a particular path and developed tunnel vision or just too close to things to see the forest for the trees. Yet to do this, we need a true friend—someone we can rely on—who won't hesitate to tell us what we need to hear, not just what we want to hear.

Inspiration

We run parallel to others around us when we are in relationships. Many of our thoughts and experiences are similar to one another. This enables you to perceive your latent potential and that of others. You push each other to greater heights than you could have done separately. As a result, we developed as a team and accomplished more than we ever imagined.

BARRIERS TO MEANINGFUL CONNECTIONS

We've all experienced the annoyance of running into a barrier or a roadblock while traveling. It obstructs progress. Often, it denotes a long traffic snarl that may go on for miles. It's typical for barriers to appear in conversations when viewpoints diverge. This often leads to defensive actions and uncomfortable circumstances. We naturally need to defend and uphold our thoughts and opinions because we are human.

It is getting harder to make and keep these vital connections with people for the following six reasons:

Depending on how you choose to use it, technology can help you build relationships and help you avoid making any connections.

- Technology can help establish connections and help you evade forming any relationships depending on how you use it.
- Our busy schedules
- Sometimes, we can't bring ourselves to care.
- We don't want to share parts of our lives

- Vulnerability scares us
- Listening to people and remembering half of what we deem junk information' is challenging but valuable when developing relationships.

HOW TO BUILD MEANINGFUL RELATIONSHIPS?

How can we fight for genuine connection in our lives and with those around us? Below, I've outlined a few of my ideas.

1. Steer clear of having superficial conversations.

In today's world, "feeling connected" is incredibly easy. We can text each other often, check on our Instagram updates, and communicate while playing online games. We feel like we know what's happening in each other's life.

This deceptive sense of connection is hampering genuine conversation and authentic connection.

A significant portion of communication is lost whenever interactions occur through text because of nonverbal cues and tone. Conversations are becoming less emotional (no matter how many emojis or gifs you use). As a result, the connection needs a significant lot of feeling.

2. Make contact through phone calls or FaceTime.

It can sometimes be challenging to hold these attentive conversations in person. When this happens, we can reach out by making a phone conversation or Facetime call to develop deep relationships.

3. Look for shared interests

Discovering shared interests is essential for creating lasting connections. Even if a relationship shouldn't be built simply on shared interests, science has shown that we are drawn to people with our personalities and interests.

Discovering and pursuing shared interests can foster new connections and strengthen existing ones.

You can make sure the connection persists through life change by discovering new shared interests. You both have a new passion for yoga, hiking, or real-life marathons. Whatever it is, it can help you maintain contact.

4. Create a habit

We can avoid making plans and asking for help for various reasons, such as exhaustion, being overwhelmed by all the options, and anxiety about doing so. We often need more time or energy in today's culture.

Because of this, developing a habit or pattern with someone can benefit your relationship.

Build a routine instead of going through the whole planning, deciding, and executing process every time. This relieves any pressure that could otherwise exist. The expectations are made plain in this way.

5. Ask questions

While shared routines and interests are essential, relationships require more than just time together to have meaning in your life. You must also feel and share an interest in each other's lives to develop lasting connections.

For a relationship to be fulfilling, trust is necessary. We can better understand one another and develop empathy by asking questions. Asking questions about someone else's life is one method to demonstrate your concern for them. They allow us to express who we are, essential to building strong and enduring relationships.

6. Listen and remember

Step one is to ask questions, but you will only get very far if you listen to the other person's responses. If you want the other person to feel safe and secure in the relationship, you must convey that you care about what they're saying.

Pay attention to and remember what the other person is saying if you want to develop lasting relationships.

7. Follow-up

Following up is the most basic, sometimes ignored, step in creating lasting connections. Following up with someone can take on several forms, such as:

- Remembering a special occasion or date for the other person and wishing them luck or asking how it went
- Sending a text message after you do something together that reflects on the experience and expresses that you enjoyed it
- Asking about the significant events occurring in a person's life, whether they are good or bad
- Expressing gratitude for something the other person did for you, their dedication to the relationship, or their role in your life.

No matter how much we claim to be able to handle things independently, as humans, we are aware of the need for genuine connection and a sense of belonging.

8. Be vulnerable

For a relationship to be meaningful, both parties must be willing to show their genuine selves and be vulnerable.

For many of us, being vulnerable is quite challenging. Many myths have been developed around vulnerability. If we put ourselves out there, we worry we'll be rejected. But guilt and fear prevent us from being open and vulnerable.

Because of this, countless individuals refuse to let their relationships grow into the intense bonds we require to be content.

Vulnerability and trust complement one another rather than being placed above each other. The more vulnerable we are, the more we can trust that we are accepted and loved for who we are.

9. Mix things up

Finally, occasionally mix things up in your connections to keep them solid and new. Consider modifying or expanding your routine, setting goals for yourself to achieve, or trying new things. You can increase your intimacy and add excitement to the relationship by doing new activities together. You must constantly make fresh memories with each other to develop meaningful connections.

WORKSHEET

Suppose you want to stop using manipulation in your life. In that case, you must first recognize your techniques to manipulate people to disregard or take responsibility for your care and problem life issues.

Step 1: If you currently engage in any of the following behaviors in your interactions with the people in your life, write them down in your journal.

- Play the martyr
- Play the victim
- Act helpless
- Act incompetent
- Play stupid
- Act angry
- Say anything you want when you don't mean it

- Throw temper tantrums
- Act compliant when you don't want to
- Act lost
- Lie about how you feel
- Act suicidal
- Act depressed
- Act hopeless and pathetic
- Act confused or befuddled
- Exaggerate or use hyperbole to emphasize issues
- Tell stories or fabrications
- Act as a divider, pitting individuals against one another
- Use guilt trips
- Shame people or act judgmental
- Use ridicule
- Looking good for the other
- Cry wolf
- People pleasing
- Act hurt or wounded
- Passive aggressiveness
- Act ignored or forgotten
- Blame others for your problems
- Act unloved or uncared for
- Kiss up
- Ingratiate yourself with others
- Act overly solicitous
- Exaggerated sincerity
- Act out of it

- Overly charming
- Act sorry for your destructive behaviors
- Act as if you don't have value or worth
- False assurances of behavior modification or change
- Get everyone angry to divert attention from you
- Keep people around you in competitive relationships

Step 2: After recognizing the manipulative tactics you employ to manipulate others to overlook your problems or avoid seeing them, you must identify the individuals you are trying to use. List the people you manipulate in your journal.

Step 3: Why do you manipulate people? Write down in your journal the problems you have that you try to get other people to ignore or address. Regarding these problems, answer the following questions.

- What are your thoughts on each of these issues?
- Why do you feel the need to use these issues to manipulate others?
- Which issues would you like others to pass over or ignore?
- Which problems would you like others to resolve or change for you?
- Which problems would you like others to take responsibility for?
- Which issues or problems are the most pressing?
- What problems make you sad or angry?
- Which problems do you want to avoid?

- Which problems do you feel powerless to resolve? Impossible to deal with?

Step 4: Answer the following in your journal:

- Which irrational beliefs prevent you from resolving each issue listed in Step 3?
- What new, healthy, more logical beliefs will you need to deal with and address these problems?
- What way of thinking prevents you from taking ownership of your issues and problems?
- What new ways of thinking are necessary for you to take ownership of your issues and problems?

Step 5: In your journal, list the new, healthier, more productive behaviors you must adopt to deal with your difficulties and issues.

Step 6: Implement those behaviors you have listed in Step 5.

Step 7: Tell people you used to be a manipulator and tell them to call you out on it if you start acting that way again.

Step 8: If you are relapsing into manipulative techniques to get people to overlook or take care of you, go back to Step 1 and start over.

The next chapter helps the readers use the skills learned in this chapter and apply them to personal conversations.

CHAPTER FOUR

MAKING IT PERSONAL

e use nonverbal cues to communicate just as much as we do with speech.

- The spoken words convey only 7% of the intended message.
- Paralinguistics accounts for 38% of the meaning (how the words are said).
- Facial expression accounts for 55%.

Conversations are meant to be fun. This cntails intimate discussions about relevant topics between two or more people. Even so, many people are hesitant to engage in conversations. They are worried about what they will say or won't be able to keep the conversation going.

Maintaining a conversation is somewhat of an art; many of us nowadays don't have it. The main point of this chapter is to help you understand the skills that help improve personal conversation and to give you some techniques to practice to get good at it.

BODY LANGUAGE AND ITS IMPORTANCE

Body language is the nonverbal cues we use to communicate. These nonverbal cues play a significant role in everyday conversation. Body language may make up 60% to 65% of all communication.

Facial expressions, eye contact, gestures, posture, and bodily movements are a few examples of body language. In many situations, what we choose not to say can say much.

So, why is body language significant? Body language helps us to understand ourselves and others. It informs us of potential human emotions in a particular circumstance. Moreover, body language can be used to convey feelings or intentions.

Although posture and physical distance can be used to communicate, the three main elements of body language are commonly characterized as facial expressions, gestures, and eye contact. While it's crucial to understand body language, it's also necessary to consider other signs like context. Instead of focusing on a particular action, consider the signals as a whole.

TYPES OF NONVERBAL COMMUNICATION

Facial expressions. The human face is incredibly expressive and can silently reflect many emotions. Facial expressions are also universal, in contrast to some nonverbal communication forms. In many cultures, people show sadness, happiness, anger, fear, surprise, and disgust with the same facial expressions. Below are the various nonverbal cues or body language:

Body posture and movement. The world can learn much about you from how you move and carry yourself. Think about how a person's posture, gait, or head position can influence how you see them. The little motions you make, as well as your bearing, posture, and stance, all fall under the category of nonverbal communication.

Gestures. Our daily lives are made up of gestures in one way or another. When debating or speaking animatedly, you might wave, point, beckon, or use your hands; you often express yourself unconsciously through gestures without giving them any thought. But, across cultures, some gestures have entirely different meanings. In English-speaking nations, the hand signal for "OK," for instance, typically communicates a positive message, but it is viewed as offensive in countries like Germany, Russia, and Brazil. So, it's crucial to use gestures carefully to prevent misunderstandings.

Eye contact. Eye contact is a particularly significant kind of nonverbal communication because it is the most common sensory preference for most people. A person can receive many messages from how you look at them, including attention, affection, hatred, or attraction. Maintaining eye contact for a conversation to run smoothly and gauge the other person's interest and responsiveness is essential.

Touch. Humans use touch to communicate in many ways. Consider the highly different messages conveyed by, for instance, a bear hug, a shaky handshake, a tight grasp on the arm, or a patronizing pat on the head.

Space. Have you ever felt uncomfortable during a conversation because someone invaded your personal space? Our need for physical space is universal, even though it varies depending on culture, situation, and the strength of the relationship. Nonverbal cues of intimacy, affection, aggression, and dominance can be expressed with physical space.

Voice. Not only what you say matters, but also how you say it. People listen to your words while you talk and "read" your voice. They pay attention to your timing and tempo, how loud you speak, your tone and intonation, and sounds that convey understanding, such as "uh-huh" and "ahh." Consider how your tone of voice can imply sarcasm, anger, affection, or confidence.

WAYS TO READ POSITIVE BODY LANGUAGE

You can tell when someone is at ease and attentive to your conversation by being able to read their body language. Here are five examples of good body language signals to watch out for:

1. Take note of adequate eye contact. While avoiding eye contact and making excessive eye contact can be detrimental, maintaining sufficient eye contact with someone for a few seconds demonstrates your/their genuine interest in conversing with you.

2. Be aware of good posture. When someone sits or stands with an upright, erect posture and fills as much space as possible with their entire body, it exudes power and authority and indicates that they are eager to converse.

3. Be aware of firm handshakes. When someone shakes your hand and maintains a firm grip, they strive to project composure and confidence. Conversely, a shaky handshake can indicate trepidation,s, and an excessively firm handshake can predict deliberate aggressiveness.

4. Watch out for sincere smiles. Forced smiles can mask unpleasant emotions, but fortunately, there is a method to tell if someone is happy when they smile: a genuine smile will cause the skin around their eyes to wrinkle, forming a crow's feet pattern. This will let you know that the other individual is having fun speaking with you.

5. Pay attention when someone stands close to you. Personal distance indicates that someone feels at ease around you if they sit or stand near you.

It's helpful to learn how to read others' positive body language cues but remember that you can also utilize these cues to support your words and make a good impression.

COMMON BODY LANGUAGE MISTAKES TO AVOID

The brain recognizes nonverbal cues far more quickly than verbal cues. Don't let your subconscious impulses convey the wrong message. Learn how to prevent these elementary mistakes.

1. Leaning back

Don't lean back and extend your legs out in your front if you want to convey that you are interested in the topic or the person you are speaking with. Straighten your back or lean in.

2. Crossed legs or arms

Some experts advise concluding a meeting or conversation if you notice one or more people slouch back and cross their arms or legs because this is such a blatant sign of disinterest. Legs crossed may also be a warning indicator.

3. Not making enough eye contact

The person in front of you can inadvertently conclude you're lying if you don't make eye contact with them. Refrain from confusing eye contact with honesty on your part because skilled liars make a point of looking into people's eyes.

4. Hands in pockets or behind the back

Although many of us instinctively adopt this posture, it can be seen as a hint that we have something to hide.

5. Nodding excessively

Nodding is a crucial communication component since it shows others that you comprehend or concur with what they are saying. Yet, doing it too often will make you appear weak. It might also be interpreted as a display of apathy.

6. Fidgeting

If you're continually fidgeting with your hair or bouncing your leg, you're sending the message that you're uncomfortable or bored. Please don't do it at all.

7. Wrapping your ankles or feet around a chair's legs

This gesture conveys the same message as joined hands: you're uncomfortable and need comfort. Avoid doing that if you're trying to get confidence.

8. Patting your leg(s)

This is a significant act of self-comfort that will convey how uneasy you are.

9. Using your phone or checking your watch

We assume people won't notice when we glance at the time or a text message, but they almost always do. Unless it is necessary, stay focused on the conversation. If you must check your phone, give a justification, such as the fact that you are awaiting an urgent message.

10. Encroaching a person's personal space.

Every one of us has a different sense of how much "buffer" we need to feel secure. Hence, give people extra room when approaching them rather than completely cutting them off.

HOW TO IMPROVE YOUR TONALITY TO BUILD RAPPORT QUICKLY

Just as you would when dressing for various occasions and engagements, you should use different vocal tones when speaking in multiple settings.

The manner a person speaks to someone is called their tone of voice in communication. How you communicate your ideas through voice is essential. You risk having your argument overlooked or misunderstood if you don't do it correctly.

Humor is one instance of a tone. A cheerful and upbeat attitude is usually appreciated. The outcomes could be adverse if you communicate in a gloomy or accusing manner. Real humor makes your message memorable by fostering optimism and trust.

Why is tone so significant?

Communication requires careful consideration of tone since it conveys a person's personality through non-visual means. When a tone is used effectively, you can establish rapport immediately. You come off as assured, valuable, intelligent, and an authority in your industry, which grabs attention and gives you the power to persuade others.

Building rapport is the cornerstone of successful communication and interpersonal relations.

The way you say something goes beyond the words you use. It's an emotional cue that frames a conversation's logical side. This is significant since decisions depend on emotion, and emotional cues register more quickly than rational ones.

Consider how you might interact with a newborn or an animal as an extreme example. You certainly have a funny high-pitched voice. Regardless of what you say, if your tone is upbeat and joyful, the baby will probably laugh, and the animal will probably approach you for a pat.

Animals will likely need help understanding spoken words exactly (apart from trained comments like sit, stay, etc.). The tone of your voice can irritate a dog, and he will likely respond in kind (sheepish or even aggressive back). The dog is unlikely to answer if you ask him how his day went.

Types of Tone of Voice

You can practice using the ideal tone for various circumstances and events. Let's examine a few examples:

Motivational: A motivating tone of voice keeps people interested and engaged.

Informative: What makes some professors so influential and well-liked by their students? Their speech tone is just one of the many causes. A style of voice that transmits knowledge and encourages personal development boosts ability.

Soft: Intimate conversations are conducted in soft voice tones. A smooth style fosters and strengthens a bond in a relationship. In challenging discussions, it also facilitates the expression of empathy and gentleness. People feel safer when spoken to in a soft voice rather than an angry or harsh one. For this reason, when speaking to a youngster, people often employ a soft, gentle voice.

Funny: Including humorous stories or quotes in your speech will keep the audience engaged and upbeat. However, it would be best to maintain a light and sincere tone rather than mocking or caustic.

Respectful: The respectful tone of voice shows kindness, modesty, and sincerity. Your conversation will be of higher quality if you use a respectful manner.

HOW TO IMPROVE YOUR TONALITY

It would be best if you didn't think that improving tone of voice is a complex undertaking; it's pretty simple. Think of yourself as an actor who first learns the script before presenting it as skillfully as they can. They give their words charm, but you can also see their facial expressions.

Tonality is much more critical while speaking over the phone because there is no visual help to the listener.

Emphasize the most crucial keywords in your script. These words will improve your pitch. Also, distinguish between statements and questions and modify your pitch for each.

Do people often urge you to speak louder or repeat yourself? If so, check your volume. Or do they advise using your "inside voice"? Try speaking at different volumes in places where you need to draw attention and inspire confidence.

Recording yourself allows you to listen to your performance with an objective ear. Also, you can manually count how many words you speak each minute and make necessary adjustments. If you're speaking at a rate of fewer than 120 words per minute, speak more quickly; if you're speaking at a rate of more than 180 words per minute, speak more slowly.

Finally, give yourself an articulation assessment. Are you pronouncing words with clarity and elegance? A further benefit of having scripts and objection responses is that you can learn them, which can significantly increase your confidence when speaking. As a result, you won't be as nervous and won't be taken off guard, which will lessen your need to say "uh, ah, like, etc."

This will boost your reputation and accelerate your capacity to establish rapport.

SPEECH DELIVERY AND ITS IMPORTANCE

While some rhetoricians distinguish between style and delivery, the type of speech should be related to how it is delivered. Delivering a speech relates to how it is presented after you have done your research, structured, prepared, and practiced it. Of course, delivery matters since it engages the audience most directly. Both verbal and nonverbal cues are essential in delivery.

You must work on your delivery once you have chosen and researched your subject and created and organized your presentation. However, even the most impressive delivery is only meaningful with careful preparation in the pre-speech stages. On the other hand, delivery can be crucial to your success as a speaker when combined with a well-planned and practiced presentation.

Your confidence and readiness can be conveyed to your audience through your delivery. Delivering your message demonstrates to your audience that you have researched and are knowledgeable about the subject. You can bring it together with excellent delivery, showcase your work, and speak confidently.

Consider some of the brief courtroom remarks you've seen or heard from attorneys on different television programs, such as Law and Order. When presenting their case before the jury, please pay attention to how they convey confidence and excitement in their arguments. How can the jury's decision be impacted if a lawyer needs more confidence in their delivery?

What Makes a Great Speech?

The fact that a great speech is brief is one of its essential characteristics. However, the length of an address is simply one consideration. A great lesson must also hold the audience's attention, be delivered confidently and effectively, and have a clear point.

These tips you may apply to any speech you give, whether for work or another occasion.

1. Consider your speech as a performance

A performance is considerably more than a speech, mostly about words. It consists of gesture, suspense, tension, and inflection.

This implies that your work must still be finished after writing a speech. Practice the speech in front of a mirror, a recording device, or a few people. After you've practiced even a little bit, you'll feel more assured.

2. Use the Influence of Eye Contact

People are more likely to feel personally connected and acquire your trust if you make an effort to make eye contact with them while speaking. Making eye contact shows confidence and authority, two qualities necessary for effectively making your point.

3. Be Conscious of Your Posture

Your posture exudes confidence. Slouching can give the impression that you lack confidence. Try holding your head steady while standing up straight with your shoulders back. However, don't worry too much; if you do, your body will stiffen, giving you a nervous appearance and feeling. Be sure to relax.

4. Alternate Your Speaking Tempo

It's crucial to purposefully change speaking styles, such as volume, tempo, and tone, when giving a speech.

When in doubt, speak more slowly to allow your listeners to catch up, especially if you tend to babble. It is beneficial to remember to pause so that the speech is steady.

If you know you babble by nature, incorporate pauses into your speech. It takes an audience longer to understand your arguments than it will take you to explain them, so decide when to pause or include phrases like "Now think about that for a bit" or "Let that sink in."

Remember that you are the expert. Allow others to reflect on your wise message.

POWER OF METAPHORS, ANALOGIES, AND SIMILES IN COMMUNICATION

A metaphor is a word, phrase, or figure of speech used to describe an action, item, or something other than what it refers to. It is an inferred comparison between two disparate entities that share a quality. A metaphor is therefore seen as symbolic or indicative of another idea, possibly an abstract one. Shakespeare once said, "All the world's a stage," which is a metaphor equating the events of our world to those taking place on a stage where actors are performing different roles.

A simile is a similar metaphor with the single distinction that the words "as" or "like" are included within the phrase to give a greater degree of being explicit. An example from a clever simile that can both drive home a point and make someone grin is that Sam was as nervous as a dog with a long tail in a room full of rocking chairs swaying back and forth at full tilt.

An analogy is another language cousin of a metaphor and a simile. There is a similarity, comparison, or likeness between the two objects. A practical comparison goes like this: "Students should be compared to oysters rather than sausages. The goal of creative education is to assist students in fully opening up like an oyster to disclose their inner riches (their pearls of imagination), not to pack and stuff them firmly like sausages and lock them up.

What Makes a Great Metaphor?

Not all metaphors influence the listener or reader. They should make things more transparent and straightforward. Here are some recommendations on how to create a powerful, convincing metaphor that you may apply to improve your communications:

Your metaphor has done its job correctly when it can take a complex or abstract concept or subject and simplify its core into something anybody can comprehend and relate to. Choose familiar terms people can relate to, such as transportation, social media, computers, machinery, entertainment, current events, pop culture, and technology. "This truck is a rock" denotes its sturdiness, durability, and solidity.

They must be memorable.

Great metaphors are words, phrases, images, or visuals that stick in your mind. A striking, unforgettable "image" will stand out and be recalled for a long time. There was a moving television commercial that mixed visuals of the devastation drug use causes, revealing their emaciated, sickly appearances, with the satisfying conclusion, "Heroin. A video negotiation training course showed farm employees fast shearing sheep while assembling mounds of wool to the side. It might not kill you, but it WILL take your life. The film then changed to show someone making a bad decision by selling his animals, with a large caption at the bottom reading, "It is better to give away the wool than sell the sheep," to underline the need to avoid making a wrong decision or making silly compromises during negotiations.

They should be easily understandable.

Great metaphors connect concepts that are relatable to everyone daily. In many ways, a metaphor should elicit a thorough comprehension, either on its own or with little explanation.

Compelling metaphors.

The best metaphors often include an amusing, surprising, enjoyable, or unexpectedly insightful element that causes most individuals to experience an aha or eureka moment where their perspective on something suddenly becomes prominent in their thoughts.

Metaphors should be extendable and adaptable.

Powerful metaphors can be compared to a presentation topic woven throughout a speech. This topic serves as a recurring foundation for other parts of the address to be made simpler while still being able to be put together at the end.

Similes, analogies, and metaphors are the most effective communication tools accessible today. Use these very effective verbal and visual communication methods to help your audiences grasp and appreciate the points you are trying to make while also increasing the persuasiveness of your messaging.

WORKSHEET

1. Your nonverbal cues and body language will convey positive and negative messages to others. Determine whether the nonverbal cues below are positive or negative (by putting a tick or an x in the box) and explain your decision.

[ ] Rolling of eyeballs

[ ] Tapping fingers or feet.

[ ] Watching the clock

[ ] Looking down

[ ] Looking away and avoiding eye contact

[ ] Rubbing forehead

[ ] Smiling sarcastically

[ ] Smiling meaningfully

[ ] Frowning

[ ] Putting head down on hands

[ ] Yawning

[ ] Wringing hands

[ ] Arms folded intently

[ ] Covering ears

[ ] Leaning back

2. Facial Expressions Exercise

You must understand how to use your face. Do this exercise to feel more at ease expressing various emotions or lack thereof with your face. In front of a mirror, use only your face to express feelings for at least 20 to 30 minutes.

Ideas or Emotions Convey:

- Content and happy
- Cheerful and playful
- Terrified, trapped, or lost
- Sad or grieving
- Serious model face
- Empty, lonely, or bored
- Daydreaming or fantasizing (happy)
- Daydreaming or fantasizing (sad)

- Planning and flirting

Focus on several options for expressing each emotion in each facial feature, including your eyes, mouth, and the angles at which you can incline your face.

3. Body Language Postures

Choose a friend or partner to role-play with, and spend at least 1-2 minutes practicing each posture or gesture together. Take turns being the performer and the observer. After each pose, discuss how it made you feel and what it conveyed.

Confidence

- Place your feet shoulder-width apart as you stand.
- Maintain a straight back.
- Place your hands in your pockets or on your hips.

Closed-off posture

- Cross your arms.
- Hunch your shoulders
- Make no eye contact

Open posture

- Place your feet shoulder-width apart as you stand.
- Arms should remain at the sides.

- Face your partner.

Nervous posture

- Fidget with your hands
- Avoid making eye contact
- Move your weight from one foot to the other.

Submissive gesture

- Look away or downward
- Hunch your shoulders
- Make no eye contact

Defensive gesture

- Cross your arms.
- Squint your eyes
- Lean away from your partner.

Friendly gesture

- Smile
- Establish eye contact
- Pose with your body open.

Unfriendly gesture

- Frown
- Make no eye contact
- Cross your legs or arms.

Are you captivated thus far? Your journey through these pages is invaluable to us and to future readers. By sharing your experiences and thoughts, you contribute to a community of book lovers. Please consider leaving a review on Amazon. Not only will it be deeply appreciated, but it will also assist fellow readers in discovering this remarkable tale. Click on the link below to share your feedback: Review on Amazon

CHAPTER FIVE

WORK CONVERSATIONS

You must be able to hold a conversation to develop your communication skills. Although this skill has many advantages for your personal life, it also helps your professional career. Maintaining a conversation can help you build good relationships with coworkers and increase your chances of landing a job.

Maintaining a conversation with a coworker, a hiring manager, or a recruiter can ensure you get the most out of your exchange. These are three reasons why it's crucial to keep a conversation:

- **Networking:** By maintaining a conversation with recruiters, you can network for long enough for them to have a more accurate picture of your qualifications. You can have a higher chance of landing a job if recruiters are more aware of your capabilities.
- **During an interview:** Extending the conversation with the hiring manager provides you more time to highlight your qualifications for the position. They may be better able to determine whether you are a perfect fit for the job they are hiring for if you have more time to chat with them.
- **Bonding:** Being able to hold a conversation will help you get to know your coworkers better. In essence, it allows you to befriend your coworkers, which results in a more enjoyable working atmosphere.

The main point of this chapter is to help you improve your work and professional conversations. This chapter will focus on two methods to help you enhance discussions at work: listening and criticism.

TECHNIQUES THAT IMPROVE WORK CONVERSATIONS – LISTENING

The significance of listening transcends the confines of the workplace and the classroom. Fostering positive self-esteem, increasing productivity, enhancing relationships, and even becoming a better speaker are just a few benefits of listening effectively.

It's natural to think of listening as a passive, undemanding activity, yet it calls on more than simply the capacity to take in information from others. Listening is a dynamic process.

Hearing or Listening

Hearing is an unintentional, automatic, and effortless brain reaction to sound. Sounds are all around us most of the time. For instance, we are used to the noises of airplanes, lawn-mowers, furnaces, and other household appliances. We have trained ourselves to disregard those incidental sounds when we hear them unless there is a specific reason not to. We develop the ability to filter out sounds that are unimportant to us, just as we choose to hear the ring of our cell phones or alarm clocks and other important sounds.

Contrarily, listening is intentional and targeted rather than random. It calls for motivation and works as a result. The best listening is giving active, undivided attention to under-standing the meanings the speaker provides. Later in this section, we will examine why we don't always listen well and some techniques for improving our listening skills.

LISTENING STYLES

If listening were simple and everyone approached it simi-larly, public speaking would be more accessible. Each listener has a unique listening style. They differ in the ways listed below:

People: The listener who is people focused is drawn to the speaker. People-oriented listeners pay attention to the message to understand how the speaker feels and interprets it. When listening to an interview with a well-known rap artist, people-oriented listeners are more interested in the musician as a person than in the music, even though the people-oriented listener may also like the artist's music.

- **Action:** Listeners who like effort focused are primarily interested in learning what the speaker wants. Do they want money, volunteers, votes, or something else? An action-oriented listener may find it challenging to listen to the details, arguments, and justifications used to support their points.
- **Content:** Content-oriented Listeners are concerned with the message's content, including its accuracy, meaning, and plausibility. When you give a lecture, many of your audience will be content-focused listeners eager to learn from you. So, it is your responsibility to provide the most accurate portrayal of the truth.
- **Time:** Individuals with time-oriented listening preferences choose succinct and to-the-point messages. Listeners who value their time can become irritated by slow speech or lengthy explanations. If the speaker anticipates a more extended period of

focused attention, this type of listener may be attentive for a short while before becoming impolite or aggressive.

WHY LISTENING IS DIFFICULT

Everyone occasionally needs help to maintain total attention during a protracted presentation. Sometimes it takes work for us to pay attention to even relatively brief communications. While some obstacles to effective listening may be beyond our control, others are controllable. It's beneficial to be aware of these things to understand the message.

1. Noise

One main thing that prevents people from listening is noise, which makes it difficult to pay attention to and comprehend what is being spoken. Here are the four types of noise you are most likely to hear when speaking in public.

- **Physical Noise:** Physical noise refers to various environmental sounds that impair the ability to hear a source.
- **Psychological Noise:** Psychological noise is distractions from a speaker's message brought on by a receiver's internal thoughts. For instance, you may be distracted by personal issues. Another psychosocial distraction from the message is the

presence of someone you are drawn to or possibly someone you strongly disdain.

- **Physiological noise** refers to interruptions to a speaker's message brought on by the listener's body. You have yet to eat and are sitting in class at noon listening to a speech. Your stomach might be growling, and your workstation is beginning to appear appetizing.
- **Semantic Noise:** Semantic noise happens when a receiver is perplexed by the word choice of a source. The speaker continues speaking as you struggle to understand a particular word or phrase. You can't pay attention to the remainder of the message while trying to understand a word.

2. Attention Span

There is a limit to how long someone can focus their attention. Human attention span limitations can hinder listening, although listeners and speakers can utilize tactics to mitigate this effect. Many teachers in the classroom are aware that when there are frequent breaks in the presentation's speed, listeners are more likely to renew their attention.

3. Recipient Biases

It's essential to listen with an open mind and to reserve judgment until the speaker has finished speaking. Receiver biases can mean biases about the speaker and preconceived ideas and opinions about the topic or message. In contrast, skewed listening is characterized by making a snap judgment and the attitude, "I don't need to listen since I already know what I think." These are both seen as noise. Everyone has biases, but good listeners have mastered controlling them while conversing.

HOW TO SHARPEN YOUR LISTENING SKILLS

First and foremost, critical listening is a skill that can be developed. Here we will review six methods to build your essential listening skills.

Understanding the Distinction Between Facts and Views

Learning to distinguish between facts and views is crucial to critical listening. When listening to messages, critical listeners are aware of the interplay between their beliefs and facts and if a speaker is presenting a message based on facts or a view.

People find it challenging to accept facts when they have an unfavorable attitude about a subject. This is not to argue that people should keep their ideas to themselves. Instead, they criticize the speech from every angle and have a bad attitude toward the speaker and the address. Critical listeners may or may not share a speaker's views, but the important thing is that they can distinguish between accurate messages and those based on ideas.

Uncovering Assumptions

If something is true, there is proof to back it up. We must still be cautious about what the evidence means and does not mean.

When you pay close attention to a speech, you can hear information not backed up by any proof. You shouldn't blindly believe that information. You would agree if the speaker provided reliable evidence that directly backs it up.

Be open to new ideas.

Sometimes, people are so committed to their worldviews that they cannot hear things that make sense and would benefit them. Because of a select few people's intellectual curiosity and discernment, human progress has occasionally been feasible despite overwhelming odds.

Always be open to fresh ideas when listening. We're not saying you have to agree with every viewpoint you encounter; instead, we're telling you you should at least hear what's being said before making a judgment.

Rely on common sense and reason.

If you're listening to a lecture and it seems irrational based on common sense. Consider whether the speech sounds credible and well-organized. Applying common sense can serve as a warning mechanism for you.

If the message is at odds with what you already know, the argument needs to be revised, or the language needs to be overstated, you should look into the concerns before accepting or rejecting the message. Typically, you can only make this choice while the message is being delivered; gathering enough information can take longer.

Connect Fresh Thoughts to Previous Ones

Making connections between new ideas and long-held beliefs is one of the most significant things you can do as a speaker or listener to understand a message.

Making insightful analogies as you listen can help you fully comprehend the content. If you can create such parallels, it will be easier for your audience to consider your ideas.

Take notes

Taking notes is a skill that becomes better with practice. You know how difficult it is to record every word a speaker says. However, if you try to write everything down, you can stay caught up and wish you had given writing and listening to a different amount of focus.

To improve your critical listening skills, continue honing your ability to spot the key points in messages to accurately capture the meanings the speaker meant when you take notes.

ACTIVE LISTENING AND WHY IT IS IMPORTANT

Being active in the communication process is necessary. To effectively communicate, one must be able to listen to another person's words while also trying to understand their meaning and intent. This is known as active listening.

The following are some examples of active listening strategies:

- Being fully present in the conversation
- Maintaining eye contact to demonstrate interest
- Observing (and utilizing) non-verbal cues
- Asking open-ended questions to elicit additional responses
- Paraphrasing and reflecting on what has been said
- Listening to understand rather than respond
- Withholding advice and judgment.

Active listening is crucial in communication because it keeps you positively connected with your discussion partner. The other person feels heard and appreciated as a result as well. This ability is the cornerstone of a successful conversation in any situation—at work, at home, or social settings.

LEARNING FROM TODDLERS- THE 5 L'S OF ACTIVE LISTENING

The 5Ls are all they need! Do you know anything about the 5Ls? It's a quick and easy technique to teach kids to listen well.

- Lap: Lay your hands on the lap.

- Lips: Zip your lips and keep your mouth shut.
- Look: Look at the speaker to signal that you are prepared to listen.
- Listen: Prepare your ears to listen to the crucial signals.
- Legs: Cross your legs while sitting on the floor or place both feet flat on the floor when seated in a chair.

STRATEGIES TO BECOME A MORE ACTIVE LISTENER

The word "active" suggests that you act in some way as you listen to people. This calls for the application of specific tactics or strategies. These are seven active listening strategies to take into account.

- Be attentive to what the other person is saying and actively reflect. This is important because it lets you think deeply about the speaker's words.
- Try not to overthink what you're going to say next. I often tune out when I have a clever, amusing retort to something someone is saying and wait until my chance to speak. But I always get more out of conversations when I listen and respond after I've heard everything someone has to say.
- Put aside your thoughts and viewpoints, especially if you believe the other person to be wrong. This trick has improved my patience, understanding,

openness, and regard for others over the past few months. After the conversation, my beliefs typically didn't change, but I did—and almost always for the better.

- Have patience. Continue to be patient and understand what the other individual is trying to say, especially when they start rambling.

- Refocus your attention on the conversation taking place in front of you. My thoughts often stray in many discussions, including random thoughts, things I should be doing, something I have to do, things I'd rather be doing, and more. I've repeatedly returned my focus to the conversation before me, much like in meditation, which has helped me develop my attention muscle.

- Don't disregard what someone is saying because you don't understand them. If you don't know what someone is saying, ask them questions. When you ask questions, you typically discover something new about the subject or the speaker. Also, it can be helpful to repeat what was said by the speaker in your own words to clarify your knowledge and eliminate any potential misunderstandings.

TECHNIQUES THAT IMPROVE WORK CONVERSATIONS – CRITICISM

Everyone hates to be criticized, regardless of who they are or what they do for a living. The unpleasant truth is that you will experience criticism at work.

Most of the purposes and forms of criticism are out of your control. However, the way you react to it is something you can control. Will you maintain your composure, or will you start to lose it?

Absolute professionalism is demonstrated by maintaining composure in the face of unfavorable criticism. This section will cover everything about constructive criticism, including how to recognize, offer, and receive it.

WHAT IS CONSTRUCTIVE CRITICISM?

We must first understand what constructive criticism is before learning how to offer and receive it. Constructive criticism focuses on giving you constructive feedback supported by concrete examples to help you improve. Upbeat, pleasant criticism should be presented with sincere intentions. To be a valuable tool in the growth process, the individual providing constructive criticism should ideally be prepared to help brainstorm potential solutions and next steps.

It's crucial to understand that constructive criticism shouldn't be seen as negative criticism and shouldn't be, either. Constructive criticism should be aimed at helping someone get better rather than tearing them down, even though it won't always be favorable.

IDEAS FOR OFFERING CRITICISM IN A POSITIVE WAY

Everyone can offer constructive criticism, but it's crucial to approach the feedback session appropriately. Try these 11 do's and don'ts to keep your feedback helpful, productive, and polite if you've never given constructive criticism before.

1. Do: Use "I" statements.

When expressing your opinion, use "I" statements to emphasize the problem and not the other person. Instead of saying "You said..." or "You did...", "I" statements start with "I feel..." or "I think..."

A good illustration of the "I" statement:

Your slides will benefit from more images. It is distracting to read the material on the page for extended periods. What if each slide merely contained the key themes instead?"

2. Don't: Use the sandwich approach

The sandwich method called the "feedback sandwich," is arguably the most well-known form of criticism. The sandwich approach begins with a compliment, offers helpful criticism, and concludes with another praise.

3. Do: Provide suggestions for improvement.

Giving someone constructive criticism aims to offer them something to work on. Good constructive criticism contains suggestions and next steps that the person may take to boost their skills development and point out what can be improved.

Examples of constructive criticism that can be implemented:

"The concept you presented at the marketing campaign meeting was extremely great. However, the lack of a connection to the process prevented it from gaining as much traction as it might have. I would present some pertinent instances to back up your approach if I were you."

4. Don't: Share your feedback in public.

Even the most well-spoken critique can be difficult to accept, especially if the recipient of your input puts a lot of time and effort into their work.

This kind of conversation is not feasible if you give your feedback to others openly. Schedule a time to sit down and converse for the most fruitful conversation. Set aside time for constructive feedback or do so at a regularly scheduled 1:1.

5. Do: Add commendable remarks as applicable.

Negative comments shouldn't be the only kind of constructive criticism. It can also be beneficial to compliment someone on a job well done. They can then devote time to strengthening their deficiencies and honing their strengths.

An excellent example of constructive criticism:

"This week, your work was incredibly innovative. It was great how you took a fresh approach to client feedback and devised a solution we might not have considered."

6. Don't: Try to force positivity.

Whichever kind of feedback you give, consider it carefully and say what you mean. Sincere criticism can be counterproductive and make subsequent feedback sessions more challenging.

7. Do: Make it a conversation.

Without a reciprocal component, constructive criticism is worthless. Using "I" statements includes giving input from your point of view. However, the individual you're providing feedback to can have a different viewpoint. Give them time to ask questions about your motivations for feeling the way you do and how they can do better in light of your suggestions. Remember that collaborative input is preferable to prescriptive feedback.

An illustration of how to turn constructive criticism into a conversation:

"I believe that this previous project's aim was a little skewed. How do you feel? Is there anything about how we're going about this project that you don't understand?"

8. Don't: Try to "surprise" someone with your feedback.

Feedback can be upsetting and overwhelming when unexpected, making the recipient feel personally attacked. Even though receiving feedback might be unsettling, trying to "surprise" someone with it can ruin an opportunity for improvement. Be careful to inform the person that this will be a feedback session instead.

9. Do: Provide feedback promptly.

Providing constructive critique shortly after the deed takes place is beneficial. This keeps the situation in both of your thoughts as being recent. Your input can be less helpful if you wait too long because it might not be as relevant. Try to respond within 2–7 days following the event.

An example of timely criticism:

"I wanted to inquire further regarding your presentation to executive stakeholders last Thursday. Your slides were self-explanatory; however, I wish there had been more time for questions. Perhaps you could send over some pre-reading the next time so we can skip the opening slides."

10. Provide feedback with some thought.

Even though you want to provide feedback immediately, you shouldn't do so mindlessly. Wait at least a day before giving someone feedback, even if you just realized how they could improve, to ensure that you can do so in a helpful, constructive manner. Consider the following before scheduling your feedback session:

- Will they be able to improve as a result of this criticism?
- Do they need to hear this criticism?
- Can I help them in coming up with ideas for improvement?
- What next steps can the person take, if any?

11. Do: Keep a cordial demeanor and tone.

In the end, you're giving criticism to aid in development. Even though giving feedback is challenging, maintain positive body language and a light tone.

RECEIVING CONSTRUCTIVE CRITICISM

You've gotten good at giving helpful criticism, but what about receiving rather than providing criticism? Even though you understand that someone is providing comments to assist you, it's natural to feel a little defensive when getting criticism—regardless of how useful it may be. It can be quite challenging to accept constructive criticism without becoming defensive.

Ideally, the person informed you in advance that feedback would be forthcoming. When someone has constructive criticism for you, you can be ready for it and avoid being caught off guard.

Even if you do get unprompted constructive criticism, as long as it isn't destructive criticism, try these six steps to become an expert at receiving complaints:

- Refrain from reacting right away. Feedback can activate our fight or flight reaction and transform an activity that should be beneficial into an exhilarating challenge. Take a moment to breathe deeply before replying, and resist the impulse to respond, debate, or react.
- If necessary, tell yourself that you can get better with constructive feedback. Even if you weren't anticipating this input, remember that it is being given in your best interests.
- Listen to understand rather than to react. Listen to someone providing constructive criticism without interrupting or defending yourself in response. Try to listen to the other person with an open mind, keeping in mind that they are giving feedback to assist you.
- Relate the criticism to your position rather than to yourself. We feel personally attacked by criticism because we believe others are judging us. Constructive criticism, however, is typically focused on your job in a professional context. Constructive criticism can help you improve your career and is often not as personal as it seems.
- Express gratitude to the giver. Appreciate the person for their time and effort in trying to help you get better. Providing helpful advice is challenging.

- Ask questions but agree with the advice. Even though you shouldn't dispute or contest criticism, it's acceptable to ask questions and come up with ideas for how to get better. It's OK if you aren't prepared to ask questions immediately after receiving constructive criticism. Set up a follow-up appointment to discuss how you can improve in greater detail.

EASY WAYS TO STOP CRITICIZING AND IMPROVE YOUR RELATIONSHIPS

Do you often pass judgment on your loved ones, friends, or coworkers? Do you concentrate on their flaws? This section is for you if you've noticed that you criticize others or someone has pointed it out.

Some people struggle to restrain themselves from criticizing everything and everyone around them. Some suppress their hurt and anger until they can no longer handle it.

Let's begin by reviewing the issues prompting you to stop criticizing others. Criticism has several drawbacks, including:

- It is painful.
- It could be more effective.
- You get unhappier the more you charge.

So how can we stop blaming?

1. Be realistic.

It's wise to adjust your expectations if someone consistently leaves you unhappy with their actions. If you don't, you're bound to be perpetually frustrated. I can't force my husband to pick up his socks, but I can adjust my expectations to accept doing it myself or not feel upset when I see them on the floor.

2. Consider the advantages.

Please try to find those acting morally upright; when you do, give them lots of credit. According to research, it takes five positive encounters to undo the harm caused by a bad interaction.

3. Don't take their actions personally.

Humans make mistakes, get worn out, and overcommit. Your friend's or family member's actions could be due to a variety of factors that are unrelated to you. Instead of assuming the worst about someone's decisions, try to expect the best.

4. Think about whether you even need to speak.

The ancient adage "If you have nothing good to say, don't say anything at all" has some truth. At times, it's best to stay silent. Before deciding whether to say something, step outside the room and calm down with a few steady, deep breaths.

5. Be direct and respectful while asking for what you want.

Even if you will only sometimes get what you ask for, it increases the likelihood that your demands will be met if you ask in a way that will be understood. Instead of blaming your wife for not washing the dishes, politely ask that she do so and explain why it is significant to you.

6. Self-control your anxiety and worry.

As said earlier, criticism isn't always about someone else's actions. You can lessen the criticism you give others by controlling your anxiety and other moods using various techniques like psychotherapy, meditation, exercise, journaling, nutrition, or medication.

HOW TO CRITICIZE WITH KINDNESS

If we're going to criticize, we should do so respectfully. We must appreciate the benefits of other people's points of view, admit that our theoretical interpretation may be flawed, and accept the possibility that one day our theories will prove incorrect or, at the very least, obsolete. The following four guidelines will help you write a successful critical commentary:

- Your goal should be to accurately and vividly re-express your target's position to the point where your target responds, "Thanks, I wish I'd thought of expressing it that way.
- Include any areas of agreement in your list (especially if they are not topics with many consensuses).
- Please share any insights you gained from your target.
- Only then can you voice even a single word in opposition or criticism?

ENGAGING CONVERSATION STARTERS FOR WORK

For professionals, effective communication and fruitful conversations are essential to success.

Engaging conversation starters are often used as the first means of communication of the day. We can hone our vocal expressions in several ways, but nothing beats a good, old-fashioned conversation!

Starting with fun opener questions or stories before getting down to business is the most straightforward approach to ensure your team members are present in meetings or networking events. A solid conversation starter is an effective icebreaker that helps individuals feel at ease and more at home in their surroundings.

We've compiled a list of the best conversation starters, meeting themes, and follow-up questions to keep business-people interested and make them feel involved.

These starters will ensure that the conversation continues whether you're looking for topics to discuss with your boss, a new coworker, or someone you've just met. These topics will start your team meeting well and keep it going!

Here are the top 10 conversation starters for the workplace in 2023.

1. Hello, how are you? How is the family doing?

2. What do you enjoy doing?

3. Any upcoming trips?

4. How long have you worked for the company?

5. How has your recent workload been?

6. What tops your list of things to do?

7. Where have you been that is the coolest?

8. Which one skill would you most like to learn?

9. What superpower would you most like to possess?

10. Do you prefer being alone or around others?

WORKSHEET

ACTIVE LISTENING

Listening is an active process that requires effort. Active listeners demonstrate that they are paying attention, promote sharing, and work to understand what is being said. Please practice using the following techniques to improve your active listening skills.

Demonstrate that you are paying attention.

Put away distractions. Distractions should be put away so you can concentrate on the conversation and make the other person feel heard. If you are using your phone, watching TV, or engaging in other activities while listening, the message is sent that the speaker's words are unimportant.

Communicate both verbally and nonverbally. Interest and empathy are demonstrated through body language and brief verbal cues that mirror the speaker's effect (for example, reacting with excitement if the speaker is excited).

Verbal

"mm-hmm" / "uh-huh."

"that's interesting."

"that makes sense."

Non-verbal

nodding in agreement

eye contact

reacting to emotional content (e.g., smiling)

Encourage Sharing.

Ask open-ended questions. These questions invite explanations rather than "yes" or "no" answers—asking a broad-scope question signals the speaker that you are interested in learning more.

- "How does it feel to…?"
- "How did you feel at that time when…?"
- "Can you please elaborate about…?"
- "How to do you…?"
- "What do you enjoy about…?"
- "What are your opinions on…?"

Employ reflections. Write a summary of the speaker's main points in your own words. Ensure you add emotional content, even if it is only conveyed through tone or body language.

Speaker: I've been struggling at work recently. So much needs to be done, and I'm struggling to keep up. My supervisor is upset because nothing has been done, but I can't help it.

Listener: You seem to try your best to keep up, but there is too much to do. That sounds challenging!

Make an effort to Understand.

Be Present. Listening entails focusing on the verbal content, tone, and body language of others. Instead of thinking about other mental diversions, such as what you want to say next, focus your attention on listening. When possible, save sensitive conversations until there are few distractions.

Be open-minded when you listen. Even if you disagree, it is your responsibility to understand the speaker's point of view. Refrain from having opinions and passing judgment until you thoroughly get their viewpoint.

CHAPTER SIX

JOB INTERVIEW CONVERSATION

Many applicants prepare for a formal discussion and questioning about predictable topics when preparing for employment interviews. However, some of the most effective job interviews feel more like conversations with the hiring manager. To unwind and be natural, treat your forthcoming job interview like a conversation with a friend or acquaintance.

The main point of this chapter is to help the nervous reader with job interview-like situations. This chapter explains the benefits of treating a job interview like a conversation and how to do it.

WAYS TO MAKE YOUR INTERVIEW FEEL MORE LIKE A CONVERSATION AND LESS LIKE AN INTERROGATION

It can feel like a nightmare in the making to be bombarded with questions and the target of a brutal interrogation. Ideally, you'll begin to anticipate it. So, I have put together a few straightforward tips to ensure you don't dread the experience or get stuck during the interview.

Ultimately, you and the interviewer will benefit when a job interview feels more like a conversation than a question-and-answer session. You might feel this is out of your hands as the person being interviewed, but that isn't the case.

Here are 11 strategies to help you ensure the interview goes smoothly, that you and the interviewer get along well, and that they remember you for the right reasons.

1. Know more about the interviewer before the interview

Making sure you are as familiar as possible with the interviewer in advance will make your consultation feel less like a formal interrogation. This will make you feel more at ease before the interview because you'll at least have a general idea of who you'll be meeting.

With so many internet resources available nowadays, it is straightforward to do this - such as the corporate website, their social media accounts, and the LinkedIn profiles of their current employees, among other things. At the very least, find out their name and use this to address them at the start and during the interview. In addition to this background information, research the company to learn about its culture, beliefs, and mission.

The more prepared you are and the more calm you feel due to your preparation, the easier it will be for you to connect with your interviewer.

2. Relax and control your interview jitters.

In keeping with what I said before about how important it is to relax, take proactive measures to eliminate any remaining pre-interview anxiety before the big day.

You can accomplish this by picking up the phone and speaking with your recruiter about any particular concerns regarding the job or interview. You can also make yourself feel less anxious by preparing for potential interview questions, visualizing successful results, and remembering that your interviewer is just another human.

Many of us find it easy to see the interviewer as an enigmatic, all-knowing decision-maker. Still, in reality, they once sat in the same position as you will in the interview room, anxiously awaiting their turn to be questioned.

Maintaining perspective and doing your best to calm any pre-interview jitters will ensure the interview flows fairly naturally the entire time.

3. Be careful of your nonverbal cues throughout the interview.

You can bet your interviewer will draw inferences about you based on your body language and facial expressions because, according to a well-known study, they can account for up to 55% of our communication. So remember that your action is at least equally essential as how you speak, especially when developing rapport and that initial connection with your interviewer.

Even seemingly uncomplicated actions, such as correctly sitting up in your chair and smiling as the interview comes to a close, can significantly impact how you feel about yourself and how the interviewer sees you.

Studies have also shown that you can establish rapport with others by "mirroring" or replicating their posture and movements. Hence, when it comes to the interview, be mindful of the interviewer's overall presentation.

4. Giving a solid introduction of yourself at the beginning of the conversation

From the minute you are introduced, attempt to smile. Setting the tone and flow of the interview can be significantly influenced by being prepared and capable of comfortably walking the interviewer through your CV.

Hence, be sure to have a reassuring and well-organized account of how your career has developed and how the knowledge and expertise you have gained from previous positions have positioned you as the ideal applicant for the job you are being interviewed for. A confident demeanor combined with an upbeat, eloquent storytelling style is the perfect blend of verbal and nonverbal communication to make the interview feel less like an interrogation and more like a conversation.

5. You must not interrupt the interviewer

This is one of the most extensive interview no-nos because, besides coming off as harsh, interrupting often may make a conversation feel jilted and even unpleasant.

Do not respond until the interviewer has finished speaking, even if all you want to say is that you don't understand a question and want it clarified.

Likewise, resist the urge to jump in just because a brilliant answer popped into your head. If you accidentally interrupt the interviewer while they are talking, apologize and wait for them to finish what they are saying. Remember that a successful conversation requires fluid flow and is a two-way activity.

6. Your responses should begin with an encouraging affirmation or agreement.

An agreement such as "excellent question" or phrases along those lines. This might seem subtle or obvious; however, this tactic can make contact between you and the interviewer more human. Of course, complimenting the interviewer's canny questioning might also help you establish a relationship.

7. Ask follow-up questions after you've answered

Even if it's just the sporadic clarification statement like, "I hope I've addressed your question?" If it turns out that the interviewer wants you to explain something else to them, this will provide them a clear cue to do so and give you a chance to sharpen your responses.

Try to show and emphasize throughout your responses how you relate to the interviewer and what they are looking for in a new hire.

8. Provide more than one-line responses to interview questions.

Responding to each interviewer's question fully and not only with a one-line response might seem apparent. However, by proactively providing thoughtful and thorough answers to each question, you can help the conversation flow more naturally and prevent awkward "tumbleweed" moments where the interviewer is waiting for you to elaborate on an answer you previously gave.

Of course, you'll need more than one response for each question, so genuine confidence and careful preparation for the interview, including a solid understanding of the business and what motivated you to apply for the position, will pay off. Another crucial conversational valuable skill on the interview day is active listening, which you must also show in your responses.

Also, you'll be able to see if you've answered the question effectively by watching the interviewer's body language, making you less prone to ramble on needlessly.

9. Use your responses to tell a story using the STAR method.

Including some storytelling in your responses is one method to ensure you provide thorough, pertinent, and engaging answers.

The world's most compelling communicators tell stories, which is not only something for children to do. Also, it can help you in delivering a more robust interview performance. An excellent way to ensure you achieve this is to follow the STAR approach, which entails defining a **S**ituation, outlining your **T**ask and engagement, describing your **A**ction, and explaining the **R**esults. This is an excellent technique for responding to questions about how you managed a previous work issue, such as how you handled the absence of essential personnel for a project or how you worked with other departments to finish a task.

This is also a fantastic time to demonstrate your ability to engage people in a conversation by telling a fully-formed story - giving your interviewer a chance to comment and ask follow-up questions about what you've stated.

10. Be sincere when responding to the interviewer's questions.

Demonstrate your humility and excellent EQ (emotional quotient). An experienced interviewer can tell whether you're using a template because of your answers or just trying too hard when you read from a script or quote previously prepared interview answers word for word.

It's easier for the interviewer to warm up to you and develop a genuine relationship with them if you can be authentic throughout the interview.

11. Ask questions too

Don't feel obligated to save your questions for the end of the interview. It would be best to ask them periodically to make the interview seem more like a conversation, but only when necessary and without interfering with the interviewer's flow.

According to research done at Harvard University, those who ask questions, and follow-up questions to be precise, are more loved by the person they are conversing with. If anything, this is your chance to continue the conversation and learn more specifically about the company's capabilities.

To show the interviewer that you have been paying attention throughout the interview, make sure your questions are pertinent, well-thought-out, and relevant.

Experience also helps; the more you use these strategies, the more natural they feel. However, confidence is a crucial skill in a job interview-like situation, and here's how the readers can build it.

THE ULTIMATE GUIDE TO CONFIDENCE BUILDING

15 tips in this three-section guide will help you in various aspects of boosting your self-confidence:

Section One: The Inside – How to Feel More Confident

1. Master the Art of Self-Control: Establish Goals and Track Your Progress

We all need goals because they give our lives direction. Life goals should be ambitious; they should both scare and thrill us.

The easiest method to accomplish our goals is to divide them into smaller ones that are easier to work toward and keep track of. Thus, whether your goal is to buy your first home, gain the next promotion, or acquire a vacation home in Italy, set some goals for yourself and track your progress.

2. Be brave

Setting lofty goals is a sign of being ambitious in life. Also, it implies that there will be times when you feel completely overwhelmed and incapable of meeting the goal you have set for yourself. Even though this is difficult, it is at times like this when people ascend to the top. These gloomy times have come to every successful person on earth. Every single one of them has experienced self-doubt and fear.

You must look within during these trying times and rely on your inner strength and willpower to follow your dreams. You can only survive this time by yourself.

3. Stop negative self-talk

Many of us constantly hear criticism from a solid internal voice. Some of us could even have a slight case of imposter syndrome.

The most significant thing in this situation is to ignore the voice. Many believe something must be true because something exists in our minds. This is nonsense! Simply put, the voice is the result of your busy mind.

4. Stop caring what other people think.

People change the world every day against the odds. People do things every day that they were told were impossible. People succeed against the odds every day and find freedom.

There is no barrier preventing you from being this. Ultimately, we are all just humans. You have a choice: give up on your goals after listening to the naysayers, or press forward with all your might. Never give up on your dreams; follow them.

5. Follow your gut

Accept your gut instincts and pay attention to them. Your limbic brain acts as a well-tuned personal bodyguard, working to keep you safe and secure.

Remove yourself from a situation if it makes you feel uncomfortable. Avoid the area if you sense lousy energy. These social encounters give the internal narrator a feeding frenzy of negative commentary. Get out of environments where your mind can run amok. You will immediately see your confidence growing if you eliminate these episodes.

Section Two: The Outside –Looking More Confident

6. Embrace your best self by having body confidence.

You can truly boost your confidence by paying attention to your body language. Be aware of your body language, not only because it affects how people see you but also because it can help you feel much more confident. Be big and powerful instead of tiny and cloistered. As a result, you will feel so much better, and it will help you develop your confidence.

7. Dress Yourself to Impress

According to scientific studies, how we dress affects how confident we feel and perform. When we dress correctly, we think and act more confidently. Thus, dressing to impress is essential for boosting confidence.

8. Be present and listen instead of waiting to speak.

Most people don't listen when conversing; instead, they wait to speak. Consider this. The two are not the same.

Ask questions and demonstrate genuine listening using your body language and facial expressions. Make them the focus of your attention and your entire world, then. If you take the time to engage entirely with the other person, you will look and feel much more confident and inspire greater confidence in them. Building trust is greatly facilitated by being present and in charge.

9. Talk the Talk

Individuals are evaluated based on their words and delivery and how they appear. A deep, resonant voice is unmatched for its ability to dominate a space.

Speak more slowly, exhale deeply to widen your chest, and let your voice be heard clearly. You can put these methods into practice. Make the dreaded recording of yourself, then practice until you hear the adjustments you seek.

10. Be Happy and Smile

Life is so short, so live and love often. Nothing is more appealing and reassuring than a cheerful individual with an open, beaming smile that exudes warmth and affection.

Smile, make eye contact with others, and savor the moment. It's a terrific, simple way to increase self-confidence.

Section Three: The Behaviors –Becoming More Confident

11. Basic and Simple Workout

In addition to the physical advantages of better heart health, higher muscular tone and fitness level, stronger bones, a decreased chance of chronic disease, and high blood pressure, it also aids in weight management and improves self-confidence. There is no denying that exercising increases your sense of self. As we exercise, endorphins are released that make us feel good.

12. Have Integrity and Be Aware of Your Values

Being in touch with who you truly are is one of the best ways to feel secure in yourself. Never try to be anything other than who you truly are.

Discovering your beliefs and ensuring you embody them daily is a fantastic place to start. Your values serve as a moral compass that will help you determine whether or not you are doing the right thing.

13. Be Productive and Always Take Action

Each journey starts with the first step. Nothing will ever change, and you won't reach your goals if you don't take that step.

Learn to control your procrastination, utilize your time wisely, and enjoy each day for what it is. You'll be shocked at how quickly momentum may develop.

14. Become your hero

In the end, we must stand up for ourselves. Being humble and self-deprecating is admirable, but there is a limit to it. You must be passionate about life, act as your leader, and pursue your aspirations. Never accept anyone's assessment of your worth or the value of your ambitions. Be sure to advocate for yourself.

15. Be realistic and live your life

What stories about your life do you hope to be able to tell others when you are old? What do you want others to think about you and the kind of person you are from your life experiences?

Gaining perspective on things is a terrific approach to boost your confidence since it motivates you to concentrate on what matters most and put the unimportant details, which often hold us back, under control.

WORKSHEET

1: Use the statements and questions below that a candidate could ask in an interview to prepare your responses to the questions in the following section.

a. Hello, it's nice to meet you.

b. We appreciate you being here today. We'll get back to you.

c. Do you have any questions?

d. Would you kindly tell us about your previous employment experience?

c. Are you a good team player?

f. When could you begin?

g. Why do you want this position?

h. We have a few questions we'd like to ask you.

I. What skills do you have that might be useful in this position?

j. You'll earn £20 an hour and work from Wednesday through Sunday.

2. Complete the job interview conversation. Fill in the appropriate boxes with the interviewer's questions from worksheet 1.

Interviewer: Hello, nice to meet you.

Interviewee: Good day. Greetings to you as well.

Interviewer:

…………………………………………………………………..

Interviewee: Well, excellent. I'll try to answer them.

Interviewer:

…………………………………………………………………..

Interviewee: Of course, yes. My last employment was at a supermarket, but I'm currently unemployed. I spent 18 months there at that job. I used to work as a school cleaner before that.

Interviewer:

…………………………………………………………………..

Interviewee: I'm always on time and very organized. I am polite and have good people skills. I have a certificate in food safety, and I can cook.

Interviewer:

…………………………………………………………………………...…..

Interviewee: This is a great company to work for, so I'd like the position. I enjoy interacting with consumers and meeting new people. The hours are fine for me, and I can work over lunch and in the evenings.

Interviewer:

………………………………………………………………………………

Interviewee: Yes. I enjoy collaborating with others.

Interviewer:

………………………………………………………………………………

Interviewee: Right away!

Interviewer:

………………………………………………………………………………

Interviewee: Yes, I have. What will my hourly rate be? What days will I be required to work?

Interviewer:

………………………………………………………………………………

Interviewee: Many thanks for having me. I look forward to hearing from you.

CHAPTER SEVEN

DATING CONVERSATION

*P*olitics, religion, and sexuality were once off-the-table topics when discussing one's life on a first date. But have the regulations and acceptable norms changed?

We no longer study the same dating etiquette manual our parents did because the rules have changed. Do you divulge every detail, including your sexual history and political beliefs, on the first date? Or do you withhold information until you get to know someone?

The main point of this chapter is to help the readers understand how conversations work when they're trying to build a romantic relationship.

HOW TO DEVELOP A RELATIONSHIP VIA CONVERSATIONAL SKILLS

Effective communication and conversation are essential for happy, healthy romantic relationships. Remember these tips when you next go on a date or have a meaningful conversation with your loved one or significant other.

Conversations cover much ground. It involves more than just the words said and heard, the conversation's accompanying nonverbal cues, and how the message is perceived. These aspects and other crucial components form a bond between discussion partners. The LOC method, which should be used in any interaction aimed at forging new relationships, is one way to approach managing your conversations effectively:

- Listen
- Observe
- Compliment.

We have previously discussed active listening in Chapter 5, so we will only focus on how to observe and give compliments during a conversation in this section.

Observation

Individuals sometimes struggle to articulate their thoughts or feelings, needs or wants, hopes, and fears.

- They may need to communicate more efficiently.
- They may be too preoccupied with what is happening to them to perceive things.
- They might be trying to conceal something out of concern for the repercussions.

Instead of only listening to what is being said, observing people in their environment when gathering information in these situations is crucial. It can clarify social dynamics and how individuals live and support or refute previous statements.

Compliment

Your new hairstyle is gorgeous. Your speech touched me deeply. I can't express how wonderful it was to talk to you last week when I was upset; you are a genuinely excellent friend.

Each time we give or receive a compliment, we feel pleased. Compliments enable us to express the gratitude we have for one another.

Whether you're conversing with someone you know or have just met, complimenting someone can also be an excellent conversation starter or a method to overcome a stumbling block.

With the above in mind, please apply the active listening skills we learned in Chapter 5. If you need to, please flip back to re-read the relevant sections of that chapter.

WAYS TO TRANSFORM A CONVERSATION INTO A FRIENDSHIP

We've all been in circumstances when we meet someone with whom we think we'd get along well as friends but end up leaving without developing a tighter bond. It might be challenging to transition from a simple discussion to a prospective friendship without appearing awkward or needy. These ten suggestions will help you establish a more robust connection in the first few minutes of a conversation and prevent you from later regretting not making more of an effort to turn a new acquaintance into a friend.

Keep no score of who contacts whom.

If you love their company, what difference does it make who phones first or whose turn it is to schedule a get-together? Sometimes people find initiating difficult because of their personalities or life schedules and situations. Some people will never naturally take the lead. Some people never start because they are so terrified of being rejected. To take such things personally is a mistake.

Be reliable.

Do what you promise to do when you say you will. Be honest with yourself and your friend if you can't do something, and call them to let them know why. When you give people plenty of advance notice that you won't be able to fulfill an agreement or promise, they are far more understanding. Nobody enjoys being let down, especially at the eleventh hour.

Even if you're not interested, pretend to be.

People remember individuals who show interest in what they have to say. Ask questions to encourage the speaker to elaborate. For more information, ask the person. Ask them what they took away from the encounter. Wait until you are sure the other person has finished before moving on to your narrative.

Ask open-ended questions.

Asking questions that can be answered in only two words makes it tough to establish a connection with someone. There is no possibility of a link forming. Ask, "What do you think of your neighborhood? Instead of asking, "Where do you live?" Instead of, "Where did you get that shirt?" Consider asking, "What do you think of the new store at the mall?" A bond is more likely to develop the more you communicate.

Employ words with feeling.

By employing emotive language, you can pique the curiosity of your new friend and establish a sincere connection. Being factual makes a conversation dry and uninteresting. Describe how anxious you felt when you nearly missed your relationship rather than going into detail about where you stayed on your vacation to London. Talk about how much you hate that hour of your day instead of how long your commute is.

Speak encouraging things.

Don't whine or complain about your life or express how disturbed you are by drama at work or with friends. It may appear that you constantly generate drama and negative vibes, which is off-putting. A potential friend will be apprehensive of getting too close as a result.

Don't blab.

Several people will respond to your blab immediately but won't want to get to know you further. They'll be thinking about what you will say about them when you are with someone else. When you talk about others, try to be positive and give them the benefit of the doubt. Better yet, talk about the two of you without including anyone else who isn't present in the conversation.

Praise mutual friends.

If you have mutual friends, be courteous while mentioning them. This will raise the likelihood that this new friend will think highly of you and will enhance the possibility that the three of you can get together at some point.

Maintain eye contact.

Everyone has some level of insecurity, one of the best-kept secrets. Lean in a little when the other person is speaking, and occasionally use the person's name. Pick something to admire about them, and then tell them how clever, funny, or interesting they are. Genuine compliments make others feel at ease in your presence.

Let people know you care.

Call the person if you haven't seen them in a while to see if they're ill or experiencing problems. Be encouraging. If you can, offer a hand. When someone returns to work after getting sick or losing a loved one, check in with them sometimes to let them know you understand that it can be challenging to return to normal. Everything is fine, but you and your friend can't get together because of general busyness? Keep in touch. Add them as Facebook friends. Email. Skype. It is quick and keeps the friendship going even while you are apart. Just be sure to return to in-person hanging out as soon as possible.

Discuss potential activities for the future.

If your new friend brings up an activity you both enjoy, ask them to join you in action in the future. Say that you'd love for them to come along surfing the next time you go to the beach, or whatever the situation may be, but not in a weird way where you pull out your phone and start checking the calendar.

Don't be afraid to ask to connect.

A friendship may develop if they respond enthusiastically to your friend request and do it immediately. Saying something like, "I'll have to friend you on Facebook," will imply that you want to be a close friend. This is an excellent approach to determine if they are likewise interested in friendship.

BUILDING RAPPORT – THE A.R.E METHOD OF REELING PEOPLE IN

Dr. Carol Fleming, a communications specialist, introduced the A.R.E. technique, which consists of a three-step approach to starting a conversation: A.R.E. stands for Anchor, Reveal, and Encourage.

Anchor

An anchor is an excellent method to hook into a conversation. How? Commenting on a shared encounter at the gathering or where the exchange occurs. Below is an example:

- "This cocktail is pretty nice; what's in it?"
- "I'm shocked that the bus is running late once more."

- "It's amazing how I got out of that line; I thought I would wait forever."
- "The last band on stage killed it."
- "Jonas' show is fantastic."

The key here is to reject the notion that such remarks can come off as trite or uninteresting. Of course, there are always more effective approaches, like comedy, but we must keep things simple for now.

Reveal

What better method to establish rapport with the other person than to share a personal story? This is the next step. Examples might include:

- "You know, Jonas is one of my best friends. We have been friends since high school, and I am extremely proud of his artistic development."
- "This is my first time attending a concert of this kind, and I must say, I enjoy it."
- "Last year, I had a similar cocktail at a beach bar in Malibu, and it was amazing."

Did you see a pattern here? All three of the statements above can arouse excitement. Excitation is a terrific technique to pique people's curiosity, get them to lower their guard, and eventually win their trust.

Encourage

The final step of the approach calls for a statement that, without being aggressive or obtrusive, shifts the pressure from you to them. Just encourage them in a manner that makes them feel motivated to continue the conversation.

- "And how about you? Is this your first visit to New York?
- "Judging by your style, you appear to prefer the Red Hot Chili Peppers. Didn't you like the previous band?
- "I can tell you detest cocktails by the look in your eyes. You prefer drinking whiskey, don't you?

As you can see, most of the proposed questions aim to break the routine of "What do you do?" and "How is the weather?" and start a more exciting conversation. This is a fundamental tenet of effective communication and might be the most important thing that encourages both parties to keep the conversation going.

HOW TO BUILD RAPPORT: 7 TIPS FOR CONNECTING WITH OTHERS

Verbal communication alone is insufficient to forge a strong relationship with another individual or group; building rapport includes a combination of social skills required to interact effectively with others. Rapport-building methods include:

1. Know yourself

Taking an inventory of your personality is the first step in learning to establish rapport for communication. You will connect with your genuine self and establish relationships with clients, customers, and everyone else by becoming more aware of your communication and leadership style.

2. Keep people's names in mind.

Remembering people's names and faces demonstrates attention to detail and a desire to learn about them. Recalling people fosters trust, which opens the door for candid discussion and effective communication.

3. Identify common ground.

An excellent technique to connect with someone is to point out a shared experience, quality, or viewpoint. This empathy is crucial for connecting with another person when it shows a knowledge of their emotions and past experiences.

4. Practice active listening.

Effective communication is facilitated by active listening, which also encourages conversations. Active listening implies giving someone your undivided attention while they talk. It's a crucial communication skill that promotes candor and openness, as we learned in Chapter 5. Someone is more inclined to listen to you if they believe you are listening to them, which can help you build rapport and a strong relationship.

5. Ask questions.

Throughout a conversation, asking follow-up questions shows that you are interested in the speaker's perspective. This indicates that you're paying attention and are curious. By asking questions, you can avoid awkward small talk and enter deeper, more meaningful conversations.

6. Be aware of your body language.

A strong foundation for rapport-building is nonverbal communication. Be mindful of your body language, eye contact, and facial expressions as nonverbal indicators. Face the person you are speaking to, make comfortable eye contact, and imitate their facial expressions while they talk. This demonstrates your sensitivity to their feelings. Watch out for body language that conveys disinterest; checking your phone or the time might show that you are not genuinely interested in what someone is saying to you, which can be bad for both personal and professional relationships.

7. Use discretion.

Good rapport can develop when a person is aware that they may express their feelings and ideas without worrying about being judged. Withhold criticism and only offer advice or information when your friends, family, or coworkers specifically ask for it. When you do provide feedback, stress positivity and encourage candor.

IMPORTANCE OF FIRST IMPRESSIONS AND STEPS TO MAKE A GOOD FIRST IMPRESSION

First impressions are lasting. Changing a first impression, whether accurate or not, typically takes time and effort.

First impressions have a long-lasting effect because they are primarily subconscious, even in the face of evidence to the contrary. We view the environment and other people through our filters and base our judgments on them because of our implicit and cognitive biases.

The first impression you give will impact every relationship you have. People are more likely to feel at ease around you if their first impression of you is friendliness, competence, and reliability. Then, they are more inclined to regard you as a friend and confide in you.

The more people you meet, the more probable they will remember you and tell their friends and coworkers about you. Making an excellent first impression, therefore, affects your networking.

The effects of this form of social capital can be profound on your personal and professional lives. Your positive reputation will spread among others.

We've all been there: you're worrying because an important date is coming. What will you discuss? Is your outfit okay? What strategy will you use to convert that lean-in into a full-on snog? Even the mere mention of it causes our palms to get moist.

Each of the examples above is a good illustration of why first impressions are essential. The significance of making a solid first impression increases when you combine their effects.

A positive first impression often opens doors. The likelihood of a date turning into a spouse would increase.

Here are some crucial resources to help you make the most of your first impression and guarantee that you are correctly remembered:

1. Smile

One of the most endearing characteristics a person may have is a genuine smile. A smile that extends to your eyes, even in these days of mask use, is crucial to your first impression and will exude warmth, generosity, and empathy. It can light up a room by fostering a pleasant mood and making the other person comfortable, welcome, and at ease.

2. Eye Contact

When you first meet someone, it's essential to make eye contact. Looking around the room is impolite and conveys that you are looking for someone more fascinating to talk to. Staring at the ground gives the impression that you are unsure of yourself, while tracing your eyes over the other person's body may appear weird or perverse.

3. Individual presentation

Even though it may seem unjust, everyone makes physical attractiveness judgments about others. Taking care of your physical appearance and dressing appropriately for the occasion will go a long way toward making an excellent first impression, regardless of size, shape, or age.

4. Nonverbal cues

What you choose not to say might convey a lot. We don't only use words to communicate. Our posture, hand movements, and facial expressions convey important messages when we share with others.

5. Reliability

Being on time demonstrates consideration and courtesy for others. The message you convey to people when you are late for a date, work meeting, or family event is that your time is more valuable than theirs.

6. An optimistic outlook

Making a good first impression requires having an upbeat attitude. No matter how well-groomed and dressed you are, it won't make up for the poor image a terrible attitude might leave.

FIRST-DATE CONVERSATION STARTERS

Dating has just become much more manageable. A poor conversation is the most effective way to sabotage a first date and guarantee that your prospective partner will have a negative first impression of you. It would be best to have icebreakers, amusing questions, questions that spark conversation, humor, and contemplation, as well as questions that go a little further and beyond the obvious. We've prepared ten first-date conversation starters that cover all of these topics to spare you from long awkward pauses. Also, they have the support of experts who are well-versed in the subject. With this arsenal, you'll never run out of questions.

Continue reading. Your future dates are dependent upon it.

1. Where would you travel if you could board an aircraft right this second?
2. What is something about you that I wouldn't have guessed?
3. What do you care about the most?
4. What is your ideal career?
5. What kinds of things give you a belly laugh?
6. What would you do all day if you had plenty of money and work was no longer an option?
7. What about living here do you like best?
8. Which year in your life has been the most important or best?
9. What activity from your youth do you miss the most now?
10. With whom do you converse the most?

The next chapter helps the readers to engage in difficult conversations in their personal and professional lives.

WORKSHEET

Each person should practice at least two conversation starters. Choose a partner to practice with, and alternate between initiating and responding. After each conversation starter, talk about how it made you feel and the message it sent.

1. "What do you like to do in your spare time?"

Responder: "I love going on hikes and being outside. What about you?"

2. "Do you have any trip plans soon?"

Responder: "I recently returned from a trip to Europe. Have you previously taken many trips?"

3. "What genre of music do you prefer?"

Responder: "I enjoy indie rock a much. What about you?"

4. "What's the most intriguing thing you've lately done?

Responder: "I went on my first hot air balloon journey last month. How about you?"

5. Do you have any pets?

Responder: "Yes, my dog's name is Max. Do you own any pets?"

6. "What kind of meals do you prefer?"

Responder: "I love Thai cuisine. What about you?"

7. "What is your preferred way to pass an idle day?"

Responder: "I enjoy having tea and curling up with a nice book. How about you?"

8. What have you always wanted to attempt but haven't had the chance to do yet?

Responder: "I've always yearned to become a scuba diver. What about you?"

9. What is your favorite movie?

Responder: "I like The Shawshank Redemption a lot. What about you?"

10. "What do you like best about living here?"

Responder: "I like how something is always going on, whether it be a festival or a concert. How about you?"

CHAPTER EIGHT

.

WADING THROUGH DIFFICULT WATERS

*I*t's normal to be afraid of having difficult conversations, but when we respond with respect and compassion, the conversations are rarely as difficult as we anticipate.

Why do we avoid having difficult conversations when they're essential? There are various reasons why we avoid difficult conversations, including:

- We're worried about being attacked in return.
- We want to avoid being mean.
- We don't want to make things worse.

Even though uncomfortable, difficult conversations may be essential to resolve work problems and strengthen your bonds with coworkers. You can build soft skills to advance your career and better manage circumstances at work by learning how to have these conversations. It would be best if you were upfront and honest in a difficult conversation in the workplace, and you also need to be sympathetic and diplomatic. In this chapter, we go through what it means to have a difficult conversation, how to go about having one, how to make these conversations productive and effective, and why it's essential.

WHAT IS A DIFFICULT CONVERSATION?

A difficult conversation is a planned discussion involving a challenging topic or unpleasant experience where the goal is to share various viewpoints and build mutual understanding and respect (rather than to persuade or win). Although it's normal to want to avoid these discussions, doing so can increase stress, animosity toward other people, and the intensity of the disagreement, making it more challenging to settle. Effectively handling them can improve communication.

TYPES OF DIFFICULT CONVERSATIONS

We've all had to engage in difficult conversations. Our emotions run high when we have difficult conversations, and we often feel exposed or unheard. There are various ways to define a difficult discussion, but ultimately, these are the kinds of conversations we avoid and find unpleasant.

The three conversations that make up a difficult conversation are as follows:

A "What Happened?" conversation

When we are engaged in a heated argument or challenging topic, many of us become stuck trying to decide right and wrong. We create assumptions about what is real, the other person's intentions, and who is to blame for the current circumstance. So, what's the issue there? This: even though we often think our presumptions are accurate, we often make mistakes. Even when we are confident we must be right, we typically have incomplete or inaccurate information. We often make assumptions about people's intentions without considering their perspective or how they see the situation. There are often more factual patterns that we are unaware of.

Examples of "What Happened?" thinking are as follows:

Whose story is accurate, and whose story is false? It's either one of us. Someone here is lying. We often forget that everybody sees things differently. While the "truth" may seem obvious, we often forget that another person may perceive a different, contradictory truth as evident.

He intended for this to affect me. Because we assume that other people know how their actions affect us, we know their intentions. Others, however, are affected by a wide range of factors, only some of which are visible to us.

When we focus on who is right and wrong in a disagreement, it is easy to point the finger at the person we think is at fault. This is her fault. But assigning blame to others does not solve problems. In addition, placing the blame on others could cause us to downplay our role in the issue.

The "Feelings" Conversation

Because feelings are involved, difficult conversations are challenging. It's risky to express one's emotions. As a result, many people frame difficult conversations without considering their emotional content. Unspoken emotions can resurface in discussion and distract others, making it difficult for them to listen effectively. The solution is for the parties to adequately express their feelings, discuss them, and recognize and understand them.

Knowing one's feelings might be challenging. Simple emotional labels can conceal complicated dynamic bundles. People often translate their emotions into conclusions, descriptions, and attributions about the other person. Blame-seeking is usually a sign of suppressed feelings. We can negotiate with our emotions, adjusting or modifying them, by understanding and reevaluating the thoughts, perceptions, and beliefs that gave origin to them. Whether they are "rational" or not, feelings must first be acknowledged as a significant aspect of the circumstance. Parties should communicate their feelings in all their complexity and breadth and shouldn't rush to judge what has been spoken. Both sides must respect each other's emotions for sharing to be successful.

The "Identity" Conversation

Some conversations are tricky because they undermine or threaten a person's identity or sense of self. Difficult conversations could raise questions about someone's skills, goodness, or deserving of affection. All-or-nothing thinking might increase a person's susceptibility to identity crises, where they perceive themselves as desirable or unworthy, good or wicked. Learning how to adapt one's identity in healthy ways and learning which issues are most significant to one's identity is necessary for managing the internal identity conversation. Rejecting all-or-nothing thinking leads to adaptive thinking. You will feel more balanced throughout the talk, and the likelihood that it will go well is higher if you can readily recognize your mistakes, conflicting motivations, and contributions to the issue. Other strategies for keeping a balanced sense of self during challenging conversations include not attempting to influence the other's reactions, instead anticipating them, visualizing the future, or simply taking a break from the conversation.

HANDLING DIFFICULT CONVERSATIONS AT THE WORKPLACE

Management inevitably involves difficult conversations, whether informing a client that a project is delayed or presiding over a performance assessment that needs more enthusiasm. How do you get ready for a conversation like this? How do you find the appropriate words at the moment? How can the exchange be managed to run as smoothly as possible?

Shift your mindset

Change your mindset instead of getting fired up beforehand. Consider it to be a typical office conversation. It would be best if you counted on the meeting going smoothly. Get straight to the point and enter with confidence. By addressing the situation positively, you will also bring positive energy to the table.

Practice difficult conversations in the workplace.

At least once a week, difficult conversations between coworkers are encouraged. Because with them, growth is possible. Holding difficult conversations forces businesses to address uncomfortable topics. And it can help companies manage them, particularly regarding important issues like pay inequality and workplace diversity.

Prepare in advance

Preparing for these challenging workplace conversations in advance is usually a good idea. Focusing on the central problem immediately reduces the likelihood that the conversation may take an unexpected turn. But resist the urge to practice or write a script. Instead, please list three goals you wish to achieve and concentrate on them.

Control your feelings

Your objective is to maintain a professional and even tone throughout the conversation. This tactic is essential when you are meeting someone you work closely with. Looking at things objectively from an objective perspective might be beneficial. Remind yourself that the more in control you are, the better you'll be able to convey the message when emotions take over.

Be understanding

Give the other person time to analyze their feelings and consider how they may or may not feel during the conversation. To ensure that they fully understand your viewpoint, clearly state the purpose of the meeting. When you observe someone struggling, please take a moment to let them collect their thoughts. If they become upset, acknowledge how they must feel and reassure them that you are giving them this feedback out of concern.

Discuss ideas together

Finding a solution is the purpose of this conversation. If it needs to be evident right away, brainstorm concepts with others. While taking in what the other person has to say, provide your suggestions. Ensure there is an action plan moving forward when you reach an agreement.

Difficult conversations can be uncomfortable and awkward. But they must happen. The secret is to approach them honestly and compassionately. By following the strategies listed above, you can successfully manage difficult conversations at work while developing your potential.

HOW TO DEAL WITH DIFFICULT CONVERSATIONS IN A RELATIONSHIP

Do you and your partner avoid discussing specific topics because they might get heated? Talking about parenting techniques or the expense of your child's services makes you uncomfortable. These tips will soften difficult conversations with your partner.

1. Let go of the desire to be correct.

Remember that the main goal is to solve a problem before you ask for a conversation. And that the solution will impact your entire family. Thus, it is irrelevant who is correct or incorrect. It is essential that the two of you collaborate to make things better. Also, remember that embracing various points of view often results in the best and most innovative solutions.

2. Pick an appropriate time to talk.

Nobody enjoys being buttonholed when they enter the building after work or in a hurry. Talk instead when you're both at your most productive. Try to talk when you both have had a chance to relax and can give your conversation your full attention. Asking, "Is this still a good time to talk?" is a brilliant idea even if you have already scheduled a time for your chat. Find a more suitable time if necessary. Your conversation will be advantageous.

3. Get the conversation off on a good note.

Express gratitude to your partner for being open to discussing the challenging topic and cooperating with you to find a solution. You may say, "Thank you for discussing this with me. It's been weighing heavily on my thoughts. But whenever we can talk things out together, I always feel better.

4. Remain focused on the issue at hand.

You shouldn't bring up previous issues in your relationship or other problems now. Even yet, your spouse might stray from the subject. To keep the conversation on track, you may use phrases like, "Let's talk about one thing at a time," or "I'd be happy to talk about that issue tomorrow." But let's tackle this issue right now.

5. listen to what your partner is saying.

Making difficult conversations work requires active listening. And to do that, you must pay attention to what your conversation partner says. Please make an effort not to interrupt them. Wait to begin formulating your following response while your conversation partner is still speaking. Before speaking, try to stay in the moment and take in what your spouse has to say. And make an effort to avoid passing snap judgment.

6. Even if you disagree, consider what is said.

Reiterating what you've heard will help your spouse recognize you're paying attention. You may say something like, "Let me see if I fully understand what you're saying.." to get things started. Experts know this ability as "reflective listening." When participants are agitated, it can help keep tense situations from worsening and bring things back on course.

7. Argue reasonably.

Accusations quickly destroy a constructive conversation. Please don't blame your partner for the issue or blame them for ignoring it. Don't try to place blame. And refrain from saying something like, "You always do this!" Why? Your partner might even counterattack if they feel defensive. Whatever progress you two were making would end as a result of your conversation.

8. Look for something you agree with.

Perhaps you fervently disagree with what your partner is saying. But do your emotions overlap in any way? Even a tiny amount of agreement can make you both feel like you're progressing toward a solution. You might say, "I know we shouldn't let Peter play until he finishes his homework. "I agree that he needs to finish his schoolwork since it is essential. However, I believe it will be easier if he has a break in the middle."

9. Take a break if you need to.

Your conversation can become too heated to continue, no matter how hard you try. Before you begin, think about putting up a timeout signal. Or say, "Let's stop for now," and arrange a time to chat again in the next 24 hours. Try resuming the conversation once you're both at ease. If problems continue, you may seek the assistance of a specialist, such as a minister or a therapist, to help you resolve your differences.

REALIZING WHEN TO SPEAK UP AND WHEN TO KEEP QUIET

The proverbial advice to "choose your battles wisely" is a sensible one to follow. Though many know what it entails, only some put it into practice. As a result, several disputes, feuds, and altercations have broken out over the silliest of issues.

You would think that the human race would have mastered effective communication after so many years of using words to communicate. Sadly, it hasn't happened. It can't hurt to pause for a moment and consider whether a colleague's comments (or actions) are worth reacting to because words can never truly represent another person's purpose.

Conflict can be avoided by controlling one's temper and using less sensitivity when confronted with a potentially upsetting word or circumstance. It also helps to know when to talk and when to keep quiet.

Speak Up...

1. ...when you must correct someone.

It's in everyone's best interest that when a coworker consistently describes inaccurate figures, data, or procedures during a meeting, they should be corrected. But you also don't want to come across as a smug know-it-all. By padding the correction with something encouraging, you avoid appearing authoritative. Say something like, "Congratulations on a well-prepared presentation, but I feel that I should point out..."

2. ...when you can contribute something.

It would be best to speak out when you have suggestions on improving your company's finances, marketing, policies, or any other part. The sooner you speak up during meetings, the more effective a participant you'll be. If you wait until everyone has spoken, you can compare your ideas to others and worry about whether you are making a worthwhile contribution. Of course, you must be knowledgeable, organized, and focused before speaking.

3. ...when you don't feel well.

Health, especially at work, is wealth. You're not doing the company any favors by showing up when you're not feeling well. Ask for the remainder of the day off or take some sick leave to recover if you're feeling under the weather because you can only perform good work when you're healthy.

4. ...when you observe an illicit activity.

Keeping quiet would be a mistake if you observe a coworker breaking corporate rules or the law. It is best to inform those in positions of authority of what you know since if something goes wrong, it will only worsen, and you risk being implicated in the situation even though you are innocent. Please don't assume it is unimportant because the company's problems will impact you. Keep an eye out for any illegal behavior and report it to higher authorities.

5. ...when you don't understand a directive or task

When working as an employee, it's easy to become stressed out by all the tasks, duties, and projects that must be completed. You can only properly do jobs if you know what you're supposed to do. Ask again for instructions if you need help carrying out particular activities or operations. Being a fool for a moment is preferable to being a fool for life.

6. ...when being silent has negative consequences.

You are committing "the sin of omission if you stand by and remain silent while a problem persists. Even though staying quiet will help you avoid conflict, silence is a method of communication just as valid as speaking. Consider what would happen if you kept your thoughts to yourself and the greater good. Even while you can't foresee the outcomes with absolute certainty, by just taking the time to reflect, you should be able to forecast how things will pan out. If you expect people to accuse you of hiding information in the future, then it's best to make your peace.

Be Quiet...

1. ...when you're upset.

You stand a good chance of saying something you'll later regret if you allow your emotions to rule your speech. Anger-fueled outbursts can ruin your professional goals and your relationships with coworkers. Even if you're right and the other person is wrong, responding furiously won't make you seem reasonable after the dispute. People won't forget, even if you apologize and can't take back what has already been spoken.

2. ...when you are sharing gossip

When your coworkers are chatting about another employee in the cafeteria or restroom, it can be tempting to join them. However, before you join in, consider how you would feel if you were the subject of their conversation. Tiny, harmless conversations can soon become harmful rumors; you don't want to be a part of that. So that problems can be remedied as quickly as possible, stop gossiping immediately or alert your supervisor about the situation.

3. ...when you're about to complain

There will always be complaints. But if it becomes a habit, it can hurt you and those close to you. You have too much work from the boss; The air conditioner is set too high; Your team needs to be more competent. The wisest course of action is to keep your concerns to yourself unless you're dishing out constructive criticism. Keep in mind that whiners are despised.

4. ...when someone is providing a solution.

You could occasionally find yourself at work in a rut and hoping for an answer. You should be aware that sometimes the most unlikely places provide answers to prayers. So, when someone approaches you and suggests a new action, be silent and pay attention. Suggestions should be evaluated based on their merit rather than the source.

5. ...when everyone has decided for you.

Keep your mouth shut if your disagreement stems purely from your self-interest and not the group's interests when there is a solid consensus for moving forward with a disagreeing decision. Put the team's overall well-being foremost.

DEALING WITH CONFLICTS WITH EFFECTIVE COMMUNICATION

Conflict arises when people disagree over disparate ideas, interests, needs, etc. One must learn to compromise with others to some degree if disputes are to be avoided or resolved.

This is when effective communication comes in. It has been repeatedly noted that poor communication is the root cause of most conflicts. Poor communication is the main factor in most disputes and misunderstandings.

On the other hand, regular and effective communication enables people to understand each other's needs, require-ments, and thoughts better. It makes it very easy to under-stand the requirements of other people and how they view a given problem, facilitating better collaboration among those engaged in finding a solution.

Below are 11 effective communication strategies to resolve conflicts:

1. Listening Actively

Simple listening and active listening are two entirely different concepts. Active listening is paying conscious attention to the information being delivered, interpreting it, and formulating answers. In contrast, passive listening can be biological (i.e., you hear the words without understanding them).

Conflict resolution requires active listening. This is because you can only genuinely understand the other person's issue and find a workable solution to your difficulty when actively listening to them.

Therefore, the next time your partner complains to you about something, pay attention to what they have to say instead of simply tuning them out. By actively listening to your partner before an argument starts, you'll be shocked at how many of them you can prevent. Please refer to and reread the active listening section in Chapter 5.

2. Documenting the Conflict

People tend to believe that speaking is the only form of communication. However, writing is an equally effective communication tool.

You can go deeper into your ideas and better grasp your feelings by outlining the issue on paper. You can organize your thoughts and feelings through writing, revealing insights you weren't aware of.

You can then explain this to the other person and vice versa so that you both clearly understand what the other is saying.

So, for instance, the next time you have a nasty argument with a family member, write down your thoughts on the whole ordeal. You can decide whether to share it with the person in question or keep it all to yourself.

3. Role-playing

This may appear strange or perplexing, but it's an effective technique to resolve conflicts, mainly if they include a close friend or relative.

You can gain a better knowledge of the other person's position and mindset by role-playing as the other person. This will also allow you to see your perspective from a different angle and point out weaknesses you would otherwise miss in your case.

For instance, if you and your child cannot agree on how to resolve a conflict, sit with them and ask them to play the parent while you play the child in a role-playing exercise.

4. Show Curiosity

The use of questions as a problem-solving tool is another approach. People often assume the worst about others without giving them a chance to explain why they feel or act the way they do.

By employing the above-mentioned active listening technique, you can prevent this by actively engaging the other person in conversation, asking them questions, and acknowledging and addressing their responses.

So, for instance, if your partner claims to be unhappy with you, don't immediately go on the attack. Instead, ask them, "Why are you angry with me? Did I misbehave?"

5. Fostering Empathy and Compassion

Conflict can also be settled by turning inside and into oneself. A successful connection requires empathy and compassion for the other person.

Put yourself in the other individual's shoes and try to view the world from their point of view. Consider this: Why are they acting in this way? What would I do in their position?

This is comparable to the role-playing method mentioned above.

6. Employing 'I' Statements

Your word choice significantly impacts how the other person views you. People often employ 'you' statements more often than 'I' expressions.

For instance, people are more likely to say, "You made me feel uncomfortable," than, "I felt uneasy because of your action.

Although it may seem insignificant, this does shift the burden of accountability for a specific action or emotion you experience from yourself to the other person.

Therefore, the next time you sit down to address a problem, try to utilize more 'I' phrases rather than the opposite.

7. Acknowledging & Respecting Diversity

People often view conflicts or fights as win-win scenarios. This, however, is only sometimes the case. People pressing their own opinions on the other person and refusing to recognize their differences are often the root causes of a conflict.

Therefore, in a dispute between a parent and child over whether it's appropriate to go out at a specific hour or wear a particular wardrobe, for instance, both parties often vehemently enforce their opinions on the other person.

Finding a middle ground that benefits both parties while acknowledging that different people have different perspectives about specific topics would be preferable.

8. Recognizing the issue and not avoiding it

Nobody enjoys a fight. This indicates that wherever possible, people consciously avoid engaging in it. While this might be effective in the short run, long-term consequences are unquestionably negative.

That's because problems tend to fester and intensify when ignored over an extended period. What may appear to be a problem at first could develop into something much more significant and challenging to resolve.

Because of this, acknowledging and resolving problems as they arise is crucial instead of just ignoring them.

Therefore, rather than assuming the worst about a coworker with whom you believe a problem has been simmering for a while, sit down with them and try to work it out.

9. Addressing the Situation, Not the Individual

Many people see the other person as solely accountable for a conflict. They often direct all of their finger-pointing at the other party.

This hinders rather than helps in the search for a compromise or a solution. It's crucial to avoid concentrating excessively on the subject individual.

Don't criticize the person directly, in other words. Instead, concentrate on the argument or conflict at hand.

Concentrate on the issue at hand and try to reach a compromise on how to address it. Additionally, good communication is a fantastic stress reliever.

10. Using non-verbal cues

Not just your words but everything you say contributes to communication. Body language, facial emotions, hand gestures, and other nonverbal cues are all part of communication.

Your body language has a significant impact on how other people see you. They are more likely to become defensive and have a wrong opinion of the entire situation if you approach a conflict with rigid body language—tensed shoulders or back, crossed arms, etc.

Use approachable and open body language. Relax your arms and back. Pay close attention to your body language during the resolution by sitting as you would during a typical conversation.

11. Stressing How Important Your Relationship Is

Conflicts often lead to relationships ending. To prevent this, you must make it plain to the other person that you respect your relationship with them and that, even though you may be at odds, the relationship still matters to you.

Make it clear to them through your actions and words that your relationship with them extends far beyond the current issue.

Take a break, for instance, if your conflict has diverted from the current issue to personal assaults on one another.

Call a timeout or say something like, "I want us to survive this because this relationship means the world to me," to show the other person how much you love them and your relationship with them.

WORKSHEET

PREPARING TO ENGAGE IN DIFFICULT CONVERSATION

Success in a difficult conversation depends on proper preparation. Give yourself time to reflect and write your responses to gain insight and resolve conflicts.

Take some private time to pinpoint the issue and consider other viewpoints.

Make sure it is a problem that merits attention.

Request a conversation with the other individual.

"Seeking first to understand" is a good way to start a conversation.

Share your personal perspective, goals, and emotions. Employ "I" statements. Be accountable for your role.

Discuss the future and what could go differently to avoid ending up in the same situation.

Thank the other party for the conversation.

As our journey together comes to a close, I hope the pages you've turned have left an imprint on you. Your insights, reflections, and critiques are valuable. By taking a few moments to leave a review on Amazon, you offer guidance to the next reader pondering whether to embark on this adventure. Your voice can be the compass they need. Follow the link below and let the world know your thoughts: Share Your Review on Amazon

AFTERWORD

All human relationships are built on communication. A vital skill that can improve both your personal and professional life is the ability to speak with anyone about anything. In this book, we looked at several methods and ideas to help you develop your communication skills and become a conversationalist.

This book's main lesson is that communication is a two-way street. Speaking and listening are equally important. Effective communication depends on active listening. It entails listening intently to the speaker, taking in their viewpoint, and responding accordingly. You can establish rapport, demonstrate empathy, and learn more about others around you by carefully listening to them.

Body language is another crucial component of communication. Nonverbal cues like posture, gestures, and facial expressions can communicate as much information as words, if not more. You can improve your communication skills and forge stronger bonds with those around you by being mindful of your body language and how others express themselves.

Along with these essential communication skills, we've also looked at ways to overcome shyness and increase self-confidence. One way to do this is to engage in constant practice. You'll feel more at ease as you engage in conversation and expose yourself to new experiences. We've also discussed techniques such as visualization, positive self-talk, and reframing negative beliefs.

Communicating well with people from various origins and cultures in our increasingly globalized environment is crucial. Understanding and appreciating cultural differences is another essential component of communication. This calls for awareness of cultural conventions, practices, and values and modifying your communication style. By doing this, you can avoid misunderstandings and create solid connections with people from all walks of life.

Ultimately, being honest and authentic is the key to improving your conversational skills. They can tell when you are being dishonest or making an excessive effort to impress someone. Instead, concentrate on being honest and authentic about who you are. By doing this, you can develop deep connections based on respect and understanding.

Connecting with others via meaningful conversation is more crucial than ever in today's fast-paced and often impersonal world. The methods and strategies described in this book will help you achieve your goals, whether trying to expand your professional network, make new acquaintances, or improve your connections with close ones.

Finally, communication is a skill that can be studied and developed. You can improve your conversational skills and have more fulfilling conversations with others around you by practicing active listening, being aware of body language, developing self-confidence, understanding cultural differences, and being genuine.

You're all set to get out there and exhibit the new excellent communication skills you've added to your arsenal. Now, talk to someone... anyone!

Please leave a review if this book has helped you gain confidence and develop healthy relationships via excellent communication skills. I'd love to hear from you.

BIBLIOGRAPHY

23 Tips to Be Confident in a Conversation (With Examples). (n.d.). SocialSelf. https://socialself.com/confident-conversation/

Admin. (2023, April 12). *Importance of Listening in Effective Communication.* IMPOFF. https://impoff.com/importance-of-listening/

Anderson, A. (2021, December 2). 7 Steps to Making a Great First Impression | The British School of Etiquette. *The British School of Excellence.* https://thebritishschoolofexcellence.com/business-etiquette/7-steps-to-making-a-great-first-impression/

Anderson, B. T. (2022). How to manage difficult conversations at work. *Blog | Haven Life.* https://havenlife.com/blog/difficult-conversations-at-work/

Anthony, R. (n.d.). Communication Power of Metaphors, Analogies, and Similes. *www.linkedin.com.* https://www.linkedin.com/pulse/communication-power-metaphors-analogies-similes-ray-anthony

Barot, H. (2022). 11 Effective Communication Strategies To Resolve Conflict. *Frantically Speaking.* https://franticallyspeaking.com/11-effective-communication-strategies-to-resolve-conflict/

Bobpassaro. (2021). How to make great friends out of the acquaintances you already have. *Eugene Therapy.* https://eugenetherapy.com/article/how-to-make-great-friends-out-of-the-acquaintances-you-already-have/

Centerstone.org. (2022, March 21). *The Importance of Connection through Meaningful Relationships - Centerstone.* Centerstone. https://centerstone.org/our-resources/health-wellness/the-importance-of-connection-through-meaningful-relationships/

Communication skills in social work. (n.d.). https://www.scie.org.uk/assets/elearning/communicationskills/cs04/resource/html/object4/object4_2.htm

Connolly, M. (2021). Manipulation Isn’t Communication. *Conversant.* https://www.conversant.com/manipulation-isnt-communication/

Constructive Criticism: What it is, Plus How to Give and Take it. (n.d.).

https://www.betterup.com/blog/how-to-give-and-receive-constructive-criticism-at-work

Cuncic, A. (2022). What Is Active Listening? *Verywell Mind*. https://www.verywellmind.com/what-is-active-listening-3024343

Difficult Conversations. (n.d.). https://www.bidenschool.udel.edu/ipa/serving-delaware/crp/difficult-conversations

Difficult Conversations: The "What Happened?" Conversation (#1 of 4) | Ombudsman. (n.d.). https://ombudsman.nih.gov/content/difficult-conversations-what-happened-conversation-1-4

DiValentino, A. (2017). 6 Ways You're Being Manipulative Without Even Knowing It. *Greatist*. https://greatist.com/live/ways-you-might-be-manipulative

Farmer, J. R. (2020). 9 Powerful Techniques for Building Rapport with Anyone. *Lifehack*. https://www.lifehack.org/articles/communication/7-simple-steps-build-rapport-instantly.html

Gibbings, M. (2022). Why Uncomfortable conversations are critical for success. *CEOWORLD Magazine*. https://ceoworld.biz/2022/02/28/why-uncomfortable-conversations-are-critical-for-success/

Gonzalez, A. (2022). 4 Common Barriers to Effective Conversations and how to break them — Transformative Conversations Consulting. *Transformative Conversations Consulting*. https://www.transformativeconversations.com/blog/barriers-to-conversations/2018/3/18

Gurteen, D. (n.d.). *The purposes of conversation | Conversational Leadership*. Conversational Leadership. https://conversational-leadership.net/purposes-of-conversation/

Hall, J. (2013, August 18). 13 Simple Ways You Can Have More Meaningful Conversations.*Forbes*.https://www.forbes.com/sites/john-hall/2013/08/18/13-simple-ways-you-can-have-more-meaningful-conversations/

Hamaker, B. T. (n.d.). *7 Ways to Make a Great First Impression*. http://betteryouthministry.com/personaldevelopment/7-ways-to-make-a-great-first-impression/

Hartley, H. (2021, August 3). *How to be More Confident and Talk to Anyone - The Rediscovery Of Me*. The Rediscovery of Me. https://rediscoveryofme.com/how-to-be-more-confident-how-to-talk-to-anyone/

Higuera, V. (2022, September 20). *Social Anxiety Disorder*. Healthline. https://www.healthline.com/health/anxiety/social-phobia

Hislop, A. (2022). The 5 L’s of Listening and Learning… *Mathful Learners*. https://mathfullearners.com/the-5-ls-of-listening-and-learning/

How Anxiety Can Impair Communication. (2020). *www.calmclinic.com*. https://www.calmclinic.com/anxiety/impairs-communication

How can I get better at small talk? (n.d.). Quora. https://www.quora.com/How-can-I-get-better-at-small-talk/answer/Adrian-Iliopoulos?ch=10&oid=18685873&share=02c5a61b&srid=h2OTRw&target_-type=answer

How to have meaningful conversations in the workplace - Barbara John. (2019, May 10). Barbara John. https://www.barbarajohn.com.au/how-to-have-meaningful-conversations-in-the-workplace

Inc. (2016, May 3). Twenty-one common body language mistakes even smart people make. *Business Insider*. https://www.businessinsider.com/21-common-body-language-mistakes-even-smart-people-make-2016-4

Indeed Editorial Team. (2023a). How To Approach a Job Interview Like a Conversation. *Indeed Career Guide*. https://www.indeed.com/career-advice/interviewing/conversation-of-interview

Indeed Editorial Team. (2023b). How To Respond to Questions Effectively. *Indeed Career Guide*. https://www.indeed.com/career-advice/interviewing/respond-to-questions

Indeed Editorial Team. (2023c). How To Start A Conversation (With Conversation Starters). *Indeed Career Guide*. https://in.indeed.com/career-advice/career-development/how-to-start-a-conversation

Intent versus Impact: A Formula for Better Communication. (n.d.). https://www.betterup.com/blog/intent-vs-impact

Job training. (n.d.). *Influence conversations by setting positive intentions – Jobtraining*. https://jobtraining.nl/influence-conversations/

Kea-Lewis, K. (2021). 5 Hacks for Becoming a Better Conversationalist. *InHerSight*.https://www.inhersight.com/blog/career-development/conversationalist

Kishore, K. (2021). Finding The Right Tone Of Voice In Communication.

Harappa. https://harappa.education/harappa-diaries/tone-of-voice-types-and-examples-in-communication/

Komar, M. (2015). How To Be More Charismatic In A Conversation With 7 Easy Tips. *Bustle.* https://www.bustle.com/articles/129618-how-to-be-more-charismatic-in-a-conversation-with-7-easy-tips

Lcsw, S. M. (2016, January 26). *6 Easy Ways to Stop Criticizing and Improve Your Relationships.* Psych Central. https://psychcentral.com/blog/imperfect/2016/01/6-easy-ways-to-stop-criticizing-and-improve-your-relationships

Mark Manson: The subtle art of not giving a f*ck and how you're defined by what you care about. Here's how to choose. (2019, October 7). [Video]. NBC News. https://www.nbcnews.com/better/lifestyle/why-compliments-make-us-feel-so-good-how-get-better-ncna1062546

MasterClass. (2021, November 2). *How to Build Rapport: 6 Tips for Connecting With Others - 2023 - MasterClass.* https://www.masterclass.com/articles/how-to-build-rapport

McClung, M. (2023). Why meaningful conversations are important for strong relationships & mindful relationship habits. - Long walks - Real Friendships. *Longwalks - Real Friendships.* https://longwalks.com/blog/importance-of-meaningful-conversations-for-strong-relationships

Nadine. (2022). Eight ways to add value when communicating. *Management 3.0.* https://management30.com/blog/power-of-communication/

Popova, M. (2023, March 18). *How to Criticize with Kindness: Philosopher Daniel Dennett on the Four Steps to Arguing Intelligently.* The Marginalian. https://www.themarginalian.org/2014/03/28/daniel-dennett-rapoport-rules-criticism/

Practicing Sincerity Through Actively Listening | Ben Franklin Circles. (n.d.). https://benfranklincircles.org/sincerity/practicing-sincerity-through-actively-listening

Psych Central Guest Author. (2015, April 12). *5 Tips to Improve Your Self-Talk.* Psych Central. https://psychcentral.com/blog/5-tips-to-improve-your-self-talk

Publisher, A. R. a. R. O. O. (2016, November 8). *14.1 Four Methods of Delivery.*

Pressbooks. https://open.lib.umn.edu/publicspeaking/chapter/14-1-four-methods-of-delivery/

Smith, B. (2018, March 14). Fifty first-date conversation starters. *Muscle & Fitness*.https://www.muscleandfitness.com/women/dating-advice/50-first-date-conversation-starters/

Smith, M., MA. (2023). Nonverbal Communication and Body Language. *HelpGuide.org*. https://www.helpguide.org/articles/relationships-communication/nonverbal-communication.htm

Social anxiety disorder (social phobia) - Symptoms and causes - Mayo Clinic. (2021, June 19). Mayo Clinic. https://www.mayoclinic.org/diseases-conditions/social-anxiety-disorder/symptoms-cause%20s/syc-20353561

Stephanie. (2022). 10 Conversation Starters To Get You Talking At Work. *Tandem Group*. https://blog.tandymgroup.com/10-conversation-starters-to-get-you-talking-at-work/

Team, M. T. (2023, February 25). *10 Rules of a Great Conversationalist. -MBA TUTS*. MBA TUTS. https://www.mbatuts.com/10-rules-of-a-great-conversationalist/

Tips for a Successful Interview. (n.d.). University of North Georgia. https://ung.edu/career-services/online-career-resources/interview-well/tips-for-a-successful-interview.php

Tori. (2023). Having a Clear Intention in Conversation. *Shambhala Pubs*. https://www.shambhala.com/clear-intention-in-conversation/

Vilibert, D. (2021, July 17). 4 First Date Conversation Rules. *Marie Claire Magazine*.https://www.marieclaire.com/sex-love/advice/a11774/first-date-conversation-rules/

Ward, A. (2022). 7 Targeted Active Listening Games, Exercises, and Activities for Adults. *The GLS Project*. https://www.goodlisteningskills.org/active-listening-games-exercises-activities/

Workplace Communication: When to Speak Up and When to Shut Up. (n.d.). Resumeble.https://www.resumeble.com/career-advice/workplace-communication-when-to-speak-up-and-when-to-shut-up

Wright, L. W. (2021). Tips for Having Difficult Conversations With Your Partner | Understood. *Understood*. https://www.understood.org/en/articles/9-tips-for-having-difficult-conversations-with-your-partner